Here's what authors, speakers, and business people are saying about …

REJECT ME – I LOVE IT!
by John Fuhrman

"What a great 'Frame of Mind' John Fuhrman exhibits! When I see how Fuhrman turns negatives into such positive power – I know he's discovered the most exciting of truths. <u>Read this book!</u>"

> **Ty Boyd, CPAE,CSP**
> **Past President,**
> **National Speakers Association**

"If life gives you a lemon, make lemonade, is an old saying, John Fuhrman wrote the book on it. If you are rejected, use it as a stepping stone to success by following the excellent ideas in John's book, <u>Reject Me - I Love It!</u>"

> **-Cavett Robert**
> **Chairman Emeritus and Founder of**
> **the National Speakers Association**

"Outstanding! This book takes something we don't like, pokes fun at it, and teaches us how to turn it into an asset. Live by the 'Rules of Rejection' and you'll have uncommon success."

> **-Andy Andrews**
> **Bestselling Author/Entertainer**

"I hate rejection, but I love this book! Thank God for books that relate to the real life."

-Charlie "Tremendous" Jones, CPAE
Speaker and Owner, Executive Books
Bestselling Author of <u>Life Is Tremendous</u>

"The powerful new book that unlocks the door to extraordinary achievement!"

21 Secrets for Turning Rejection into Direction

REJECT ME –
I LOVE IT!
JOHN FUHRMAN

Copyright © 1997 by John Fuhrman
ISBN 0-938716-28-X

LCCN: 96-077533

Published by
SUCCESS PUBLISHERS
One Oakglade Circle
Hummelstown, PA 17036
(717) 566-0468

Manufactured in the United States of America

DEDICATION

This book is dedicated to my wife Helen, and my children, John and Katie. To the memory of my mom, Kitty. To all those who have allowed me to speak to them over the years. To everyone who needs to deal with rejection to move-on. And especially to my hero...my Dad, who taught me the "Rules."

Contents

Part Three
YOUR INVINCIBLE ROOF

Part Four
YOUR UNLIMITED SKY

Acknowledgments

When I began putting words on paper, I thought of it as a lonely endeavor. But by the time the book was almost ready for printing, I realized nothing could be further from the truth. There are so many people whose influence is reflected in these pages that it would be untrue to say this work is totally my own.

It began with my parents, John and Kitty, who let me imagine and encouraged me to dream. Their discipline, blended with love, enabled me to select words with great care and stick to the project when the words stopped coming for a while.

To my brothers, Pete and Greg, who instilled the spirit of competition inside me to excel in my own way. The constant challenges they gave me created new limits right when I thought I had reached my maximum potential.

To my wife, Helen. She never read a single page until it was complete. Yet each struggle for the right words was met with her encouragement and confidence in my ability. After 18 years of married life, with her support, I feel more invincible than ever. I am thankful for each day I have Helen to share my successes with.

To my son, John and my daughter, Katie – The ultimate successes. These two bundles of energy are my reasons for striving towards excellence. John has taught me that just playing the game is joy enough. Sometimes I forget he's only a child but I know he'll remind me. The princess can do no wrong. Katie has the knack of putting my world in perspective, with just her smile. They are my constant reminder that I need to practice what I preach.

To my editors and publishers, who are a lot more to me. Most publishers are entities and bottom lines, mine are my friends. They took each submission of what I thought was

6

my best, sent it back, and helped me do better. They often helped the words flow through my fingers and onto paper. They left messages on my answering machine, sent letters of encouragement, and always focused on my dream. They had visions of helping a lot of people and were patient with me until I realized the importance of the message.

And finally, to thank God for all He has given me – my talents, relationships, knowledge, courage, and mostly for giving me the vision to see this project as if it had been completed. His inspiration helped me to focus on the big dream – helping others in the realization of their full potential.

INTRODUCTION

"Look for ways to create value from any experience."
Susan Jeffers, Ph.D.

Those of you perceptive enough to purchase this book have already noticed it's not very big. Yet you will find the content of great importance. Consider that elephants are afraid of mice and some 250 pound linebackers are afraid of spiders. Realize also that 99.9% of the population is paralyzed, at least some of the time, by the fear of rejection! While it is but a word, the power of its ability to limit us, if we let it, is as big as a mountain.

We are going to focus on what may be a small but powerful reality of our daily lives. Some of us manage to overcome it some of the time, while many of us do everything we can to avoid it. A small percentage of us have even mastered it to the point where we actually embrace it. That is where I hope to take all of you who are open-minded enough to read these few pages, and take control of your fear of rejection for the rest of your lives.

"The journey of a thousand miles begins with a single step," says the old Chinese proverb. Life is a journey and this book deals with one of its greatest stumbling blocks. You are about to learn what I call the "21 Secrets for Turning Rejection into Direction." This process will expose you to the power that rejection has and how to use it to your advantage.

After reading the book, you can use the 21 secrets as an easy reference. You can skip around to the topics that are most helpful to you in any given situation. You will be empowered so that NO REJECTION CAN STOP YOU!

Rejection. It looms largely over many of us. Yet, in its simplest form, it consists of only a consonant and a vowel. It's one of the smallest words in the English language, yet one that has shaped the destinies of entire populations. It's the word "NO"! Just reading it creates a tightness of the stomach in some, and shortness of breath in many. But for those who have mastered it, it fosters a sense of anticipation of greatness as soon as it is heard.

Funny though. You would think, like other things in life we are comfortable with and even take for granted, we would get used to rejection. I've heard it said, that by the time we're 18, we have heard "NO" over 150,000 times! Yet we may still get the same feeling as many people do, when they hear "fingernails being pulled across a chalkboard" when we merely think of rejection. Why is that? Perhaps it's a deep-seated psychological reason, a lack of self-esteem (the respect you *feel* for yourself), or something else. No matter what the reason is, I know how you can use rejection to your advantage. That's what this book is all about.

Fire is harmful unless it is controlled. Then it provides warmth, enables us to cook, and sets a romantic tone when contained in a fireplace. Your response to rejection is the same way. When your response is unbridled, it can devastate. When your response is controlled, it can be used to motivate you, stir you into action, and bring you closer to your goals. You just need to know how to respond to rejection so that it's to your advantage. And that's where this book comes in. Consider it your "owners manual" for rejection.

Part One

YOUR
BASIC
FOUNDATION

N

Chapter 1

NOBODY'S PERFECT
The First Secret of the NO REJECTION Process

"It's impossible to fail completely and it's impossible to succeed perfectly."

Robert H. Schuller

How's Perfection Related to Rejection?

How many times have you heard, "Nobody's Perfect"? There's no such thing as a human being with perfect thoughts and actions. Nonetheless, we were created to have meaning and be successful. Unfortunately, many people use the expression, "I'm not perfect," as an excuse not to succeed! How many times have *you* said it when someone points out a mistake you've made? It's true, our thoughts and behavior aren't perfect; there's always room for at least a little improvement. Have we convinced ourselves that since we don't do things perfectly, we can't achieve maximum success? As world famous professional speaker, Zig Ziglar says, "Failure is not a person, it's just an event." So how does this tie in with rejection? They're strongly related and here's how.

Look at what might be considered the most "perfect" of all human "rejection" – birth! A child can't be born naturally until the mother "rejects" that "foreign" body from her own. The instant the umbilical cord is cut, in most cases, you have a "perfect" human being – a person who is born to succeed! Regardless of a newborn's outward appearance, it is a creation of beauty and perfection.   In fact, all living organisms were originally designed to operate to perfection and be successful because God doesn't make any junk! People are nourished not only with nutritional food but also with love and encouragement.   Once a baby begins to comprehend and move around, however, the "programming" to fail begins. As Zig Ziglar says, "We were born to succeed but conditioned to fail."

What Happens As a Child Grows?
"No" this. "No" that. You will never be this. You could never do that. Hate them. Don't play with those kids. Our family was never known for being smart.   Don't get your hopes up. Sit down and shut up. You'll never amount to anything.   And on–and–on it goes.   What portion of our imperfect thoughts and behavior is a result of well-intentioned programming, and what is human nature?

Many of us talk to ourselves to change habits and achieve goals, so how come we don't approach perfection when usually that's what we're seeking?

When you see a child hanging upside down from a tree branch with a big smile on their face, you might say they have no fear. When they walk up to a total stranger and ask how come they have to be in a wheelchair, why do we get a sinking feeling in our stomach? Is it because we were taught something they weren't? Given a choice, I would rather not have learned to be afraid of total honesty, curiosity, or to have the fear of having too much fun. How about you?

Most of us heard a lot of negative things as we grew up. We may have also learned prejudice, complacency, and yes, we probably even learned to fear rejection. Most of us were taught that some people were just better than us and there was nothing we could do about it. You may have learned that if you tried to be equal and accepted, you would only be disappointed by the rejection. Other people would laugh at you and you would be rejected from the group. You would end up alone. All this made you feel less respect for yourself. The comparison and value judging hurt your self-esteem.

As a Child, Were You Expected To Be Perfect?

Harold S. Kushner, author of *How Good Do We Have TO Be?* explains a scenario that may be true for many of us – "If we were afraid to make a mistake because we have to maintain the pretense of perfection, it is because we still remember the bitter taste of parental disappointment, of a teachers criticism or sarcasm, every time we did something wrong, ..."

To move-on we need to realize our parents and teachers, who may not have been able to accept their own imperfections, might have rejected us when we made mistakes. Then we may have rejected ourselves! To avoid their rejection, we may have gotten caught up in expecting perfection from ourselves.

Remember, our role models were just doing the best they could with their level of awareness! As we accept that, forgive them, let it go, and move-on – we can create new beginnings. Frankly, not expecting perfection from ourselves or others generates a lot more peace of mind and a lot less disappointment!

Looks Are Often Deceiving

Be careful not to compare how insecure you may feel about yourself on the inside with how polished others may look on the outside. The more "perfect" another person appears to be, the more likely they are to feel inadequate. They may be trying to be "perfect" to feel "worthy." No one has their "act together" totally. And often people are emotionally hurting to one degree or another. The more personally developed a person is, the more likely they are to admit they've got lots of flaws and a number of difficulties to overcome. You're not alone.

Again I'll quote Kushner, "It ought to be with a sense of relief, not a sense of compromise and reluctance, that we come to the conclusion that we are not and never will be perfect. We are not settling for mediocrity. We are understanding our humanity, realizing that, as human beings, the situations we face are so complex that no one could possibly be expected to get them right all the time." So it's important to accept the imperfections of yourself and others. Do your best, take responsibility for what you do, fine-tune, and keep on keeping on.

Is Perfection Reachable?

Can we really attain perfection? No! Since no mere mortal has ever done that before, I don't believe so. I'm certain, however, only those who do their best to develop their thinking and behavior will ever truly succeed. However, *excellence* is within your reach. I hope this book will serve as one of the steps in the direction toward perfection (excellence), for those who wish to make the journey. We'll explore how fear of rejection can hold you back, and how you can use rejection to propel you on your way toward the success you were destined to have.

No Pain, No Gain?

Some fitness people used the phrase, "No pain, no gain," almost as a battle cry. They've found that when you push your body beyond its comfort limits, there will be some temporary pain. If you aren't experiencing some discomfort, you aren't going to realize any growth. Mentally we need to do the same thing. To develop ourselves as people, we need to experience some discomfort. We need to stretch our thinking in new directions. Just like when we physically exercise, we may mentally move in a direction that doesn't give us the results we want. Or we might push our thinking beyond our current level of development. At that point, we're likely to experience some emotional pain.

If you're working out to prepare for an athletic competition and you feel pain, would you automatically quit? No! You'd probably take a break to heal to prevent further injury. Then you'd get right back to your regular training program. Of course, it's likely you'd make some adjustments in your routine to prevent the same injury from happening again. Likewise, we sometimes need to take a mental step back and make adjustments in our thinking as well.

Your own life is your competition. Yet how many times have you felt discomfort doing something you believed in and instead of making adjustments to do it again, you got discouraged and quit? I will never claim rejection never causes any pain. But like physical pain, it goes away. Also like physical pain, when you make adjustments you can prevent the same thing from happening again. When you force yourself to make adjustments and continue growing, you will get stronger and achieve your dreams and goals sooner.

*"Better to do something imperfectly than to do nothing
flawlessly."*
Robert H. Schuller

O

Chapter 2

OPEN UP TO REJECTION
The Second Secret of the NO REJECTION Process

"You'll miss 100% of the shots that you never take."

Wayne Gretsky

How Has Rejection Benefited You?

If you think about being rejected, like most people, do you fill your head with negatives? Yet, without the loving rejection of your curiosity as a child, you may have had a lot of pain and scars from burns from being allowed to touch a hot stove. You might not even be alive if you had been allowed to play in traffic! As an adult you might have taken a job you would have eventually despised if you hadn't been rejected in the interview process. That rejection probably caused you to move-on to something more suitable where you could accomplish more.

These are just a couple of examples of how you have already *benefited* from rejection. By understanding that *all rejection is beneficial,* you'll be able to open-mindedly examine each rejection rather than allowing negativity to creep in and take over.

Look for some benefit in every rejection. Sometimes either the person who rejected you or a friend will tell you it was for the best. This is true because *what happens to you happens for you.* That is seldom pleasant to hear immediately after someone has said, "no." But open your mind and let some time pass. After a bit you will see the bigger picture and how the rejection actually benefited you in some way!

Perhaps the rejection causes you to become more committed to your goal or dream. You may even find a compelling reason for the rejector to change their mind and give you a positive response. The key to any of this happening is that you need to reflect on the situation with an open mind, considering all the possibilities.

The Third Party Plan

One way to successfully find the benefit in any rejection is the "third party plan." When you ask someone you respect to evaluate your situation, it can help you discover the benefit, fine-tune your skills, if necessary, and move-on. Here's a story to help prove the point.

Several years ago I hired a salesperson (we'll call him Jim) to sell cars at a dealership I was managing. This was a large, successful operation selling over 400 cars per month.

In that area of the country, George Washington's birthday week is a great time for sales. Every salesperson looks forward to it because they know there's a lot of commissions to be made. Jim was a member of a new class of trainees that was to be ready to sell in time for the big week.

I was the sales manager in charge of training. It was my job to get these new people ready to face the onslaught of customers. As the class progressed, I began noticing something special about Jim. To this day I can't tell you what it was I saw, but I knew he was destined to succeed. However, he almost missed his chance. He came close to letting rejection get the best of him.

As soon as class ended, Jim met with his first customer. He was nervous and went totally blank. By the time I got there to help, the customer was gone. I told Jim to accept it and let it go since the majority of customers will tell you "no" anyway.

The results of the rest of the month indicated he must have broken the individual record for number of "noes." I had not seen anything like it up until that time in my career, nor have I seen anything like it since. Jim spoke to about 100 people and didn't sell a single car! Naturally, he wanted to quit. He was willing to give in and let the "noes" from just 100 people control his life.

Jim came to me and let me know that the car business just wasn't for him. He said he needed to get on with his life and go out and earn a living. "So," he said, "I quit."

However, I refused to accept his solution to what happened. I told him that if he left now, he would probably let rejection control him the rest of his life. I helped him change his focus from the individual customer's rejection to the "big picture."

I helped Jim focus on what he *wanted*. Once he was able to tell me what it was he truly wanted in life, I told him that in order to attain it, he would need to *grow through* (not just go through) a lot of rejection. Like other salespeople in similar situations, Jim quickly reminded me that no one had said "yes" to him about buying a car. However, I felt he was looking for a reason to stay, and I needed to come up with one fast.

I explained to him that all selling is just a "numbers game," but he didn't understand the law of averages. I explained that 100 "noes" without a "yes" is a bit unusual. But by sticking with it and fine-tuning his approach, he'll find the law of averages will eventually come out in his favor. He needed to *get through the "noes" to get to the "yesses."*

I was helping Jim mold his future, and I had a strong feeling he could achieve great things. He just needed someone to encourage him. I told him that the average salesperson sells only about 20% of the customers that come in. Therefore, he was practically due and entitled to sell the next 25 people he talked to!

To be honest, Jim didn't exactly achieve those results. Nevertheless, he soon began selling cars. Since then he has out sold nearly the entire staff everywhere he has worked. In fact, he is now a manager, helping others to keep persevering and not give up on themselves because of rejection. We stay in touch a lot, helping each other grow and work through various challenges. I don't let rejection control me and Jim doesn't either.

There are thousands of "Jims" (both men and women) out there. Perhaps you are one of them. Better still, perhaps you're the one who can help someone like Jim learn not only how to deal with rejection, but conquer it and use it to grow. Either way, you need to be a "looker." If you're letting rejection control you, *look* for someone to help you *grow through it*. Once you have overcome rejection, *look* for those who need your knowledge and experience. Use what you know to help them, and both of you will grow.

You Get What You Focus On

Once you understand that all rejection is beneficial, you can stop assuming it's negative. This outlook will help you press-on regardless of what you imagine the outcome might be.

It seems negative thinking people have clouded vision; all they see are obstacles. They are beaten before they begin. With nothing but defeat on the horizon of their mind, is it any wonder defeat becomes their reality?

Positive thinking people use rejection to motivate them. This attitude allows them to always be at their best, regardless of the result.

The "bottom line" is *you get what you focus on.*

Look at your objective through your eyes only, not the eyes of someone without a vision for their future. Measure your success by the people your plan (or whatever it is you're sharing) will help, not by the people who want to drag you down. They're not in your shoes. Don't concern yourself with people telling you how it could be hurtful to you to proceed further with what you're doing and that you can't do it. They may not want you to get ahead and may be negative about any progressive move you make.

Those without vision can't see much beyond today. Their todays are often filled with the same old boring routine – "Same old, same old," they may say. Proof for them is often measured by instant gratification, but ideas that benefit the world are never accepted instantly. People with no vision never allow themselves to see the true benefits of change. They can't see the possibilities of the future. Whenever you do anything new, you can be certain some people will reject you or your idea. As it says in the *Bible,* "Where there is no vision, the people perish." Hang on to your vision.

The only way to avoid rejection is to do nothing and have no contact with the outside world. No one reading this book fits that category! It can help you grow through rejection, which you probably knew, at least subconsciously, when you purchased it.

One of the outcomes of change is rejection, and it's all to your benefit! The fact that you are choosing to move-on means you are rejecting the old ways and embracing the new opportunity!   As you learn to appreciate rejection as a learning experience, your results can be dramatic.

"We conquer by continuing."
George Matheson

"Be like a postage stamp — stick to one thing until you get there."
Josh Billings

"I have always been pushed by a negative.... The apparent failure of a play sends me back to my typewriter that very night, before the reviews are out. I'm more compelled to get back to work than if I had a success."
Tennessee Williams

Part Two

YOUR

SUPPORTING

STRUCTURE

R

Chapter 3

REJECTION AVOIDANCE IS DANGEROUS

The Third Secret of the NO REJECTION Process

"Life is a highway – the enjoyment you get depends on the lane you choose."

John Fuhrman

Did You Ever Let a Dream Die to Avoid Rejection?

Have you ever had an idea that could have accelerated your success, but you didn't take advantage of it because you wanted to avoid rejection? Here's an example.

There was a man who lived every day with one consuming dream – to become an actor. All he needed was parts to play. Undaunted, his dream drew him to write his own part.

He put together a script and began looking for someone to produce it. He went from agent to agent and studio to studio; but no matter what he did, nothing came of it. He was turned down over a thousand times! Even if he had given up here, most people would still have called him courageous because he kept going in spite of all the rejection. But that's not where the story ends.

Finally, somebody liked his script. The timing couldn't have been better; he was flat broke. Yet because his dream to be an actor was so great, he turned down the $100,000 he was offered for his script – the producer wanted someone else to play *his part!* He kept searching until he got exactly what he wanted; he eventually starred in the movie he wrote, and won an Oscar. It was then followed by four sequels! For holding on to his dream and turning down the initial $100,000 buyout offer, he now gets several million dollars per picture.

What would have happened if Sylvester Stallone had avoided rejection? Nobody would have ever known who "Rocky" was!

Rejections Lead to Success

How would you deal with the following rejections and keep going as this famous man did?

- ◆ The love of your life dies.
- ◆ You fail at business.
- ◆ You fail at getting elected to local government.
- ◆ You open a legal practice, and fail.
- ◆ You run for federal office, and fail.
- ◆ You run for Vice President, and fail.
- ◆ You get elected to a local government position, but lose the re-election.

With all of these setbacks, most people would have understood and forgiven this man if he had entered private life, never to be heard from again. Yet, even when he became ultimately successful, his own advisors considered him to be not much more than a country bumpkin with no leadership ability. What would have happened to America had Abraham Lincoln lived his life avoiding rejection? Shatter the thought!

Rejections Kept Coming In

Consider the rejection letters received by your author.

Publisher 1 – "No thank you."   Feb. 1988

Publisher 2 – "Not our type of book."   Feb. 1989

Publisher 3 – "No!"   June 1989

Publisher 4 – "Nice job, no way."   July 1989

Publisher 5,6,7,8,9,10,11 – "No, No, No..." Aug 89–June 93

These publishers turned down an idea for publication. Had I heeded any of those letters or taken them personally, it is unlikely any of you would be reading this. You wouldn't have had the opportunity to benefit from what I've learned about dealing with rejection.   If I had avoided rejection, I would never have had the opportunity to work with the publisher who ultimately made this book and my dream a reality.

Avoiding Rejection Endangers Your Dreams

It's perfectly natural to avoid danger. However, it has become dangerously acceptable to avoid rejection. The fear of rejection is what keeps many of us working at jobs we hate. We may not be paid what we're worth because we fear the boss will say "no" to our request for a raise, and there will be dire consequences. Worst of all, we justify those feelings by telling ourselves we don't want the pressure that a raise and its increased responsibility would bring. Who really wants a raise? The government is going to get most of it anyway! What a lame excuse, yet we may let our fear cause us to make rationalizations (telling ourselves "rational lies") all too often.

Most of us have a terrible fear of rejection. We bask in the security of doing our best to have everyone like us. This is a great trap. Pleasing people to gain acceptance just doesn't work! We may refuse to accept the fact that no matter what we do, everyone won't like us or what we do or don't do. During our "MAKE-A-LIVING" training program (we'll discuss this more later on) we are told various things to change our behavior. We've probably heard things like, "Don't make waves," or "Look before you leap," and how about "You're just a dreamer."

Words create feelings and feelings affect the way we behave. Some words have an obvious, immediate effect, while most others affect us in more subtle ways, often without us even realizing it. Words are powerful and help shape our destiny.

Whether we want to admit it or not, at one time or another, our lives have been ruled by the committee of "THEY." It's likely some of the decisions we made in the past were based on the "fact" that "everyone" was either doing, wearing, drinking, driving, smoking, or living it.

Submitting to fear and avoiding rejection takes away our freedom to dream. If we don't nurture our own dreams and desires, we let others dream for us, and we follow them like sheep. We find ourselves stuck in the middle of a flock, automatically changing directions with the others and never stepping out on our own. That's not a happy thought for me. How about you?

Do You Follow the Crowd?

If you don't believe people often act like sheep, drive Route 95 North leaving New York City. You'll see one of the widest lines of tollbooths you could imagine. On any given day I can almost guarantee you will see two things that prove this point. You'll see an incredibly long line of cars at several of the lanes, which doesn't prove much. But, look at the entire picture; see all of the lanes.   You'll probably see at least one that has a green light with no cars passing through!   That's often because of the fear of rejection. Most people would rather follow the crowd and wait in line in "safety." They won't risk the embarrassment of maybe being told that they shouldn't be at the tollbooth with no line! The result of choosing that lane is the potential of breezing through and getting to their destination that much sooner.

You can become part of the crowd and do nothing different, or you can do something on your own and create crowds to follow you.

Go For Rejection and Expand Your Life

Up to this point we have been dwelling mostly on the negatives associated with rejection.   If we focus on the negative aspect of anything, there is a danger we'll settle in and do nothing about it.   So from here on I will give you positive reasons to stretch and risk rejection.

When we feed ourselves full of possibilities, we gain courage. And, even in small amounts, courage begins to displace fear. Most of us want to experience life to the fullest, and not let fear hold us back. To do so we need to become childlike (not childish) again – full of wonder without fear.

As a child, were you told not to climb trees because you might fall? Did you climb trees anyway? If so, can you remember the exhilaration you felt when the breeze hit your face and the view went on "forever"? You experienced that uplifting feeling, not because you didn't pay attention to the warning. Your desire to conquer the tree and experience the view enabled you to overcome your fear of falling. Remember who you "became" as you sat perched on a high branch? You may have been a scout looking for the enemy over the next ridge. Perhaps you were a prince or princess looking over your castle. Or maybe you were an explorer, spying down on an ancient village full of treasure. How was *your* imagination stirred by that experience?

When you overcome "rejection avoidance," you can become and do all kinds of wonderful things. When you continue exploring your possibilities, great ideas emerge that can benefit both you and others in a big way.

Have You Been Rejected Enough to Be Successful?

Every lasting success involves overcoming rejection. The only reason you may not yet be as successful as you want to be may be because, ironically, you haven't been rejected enough! When you adopt this attitude towards rejection, you'll find the rejection you face not only passes and fades in your memory, but *also brings you closer to the success you deserve to have.*

Take Your Shot and Go For It!

Whether they believe it or not, most people, at some level, want to make a positive difference. To enjoy following through on that desire and do what you need to do to make a difference, you need to face rejection. Those who don't, fade away into the sea of insignificance. Those who do face rejection squarely and deal with it, become leaders, mentors, and crowd attracters. They go through life making a lasting difference, and are constantly setting an example for future generations to follow. Unfortunately, so do those who hide from rejection. They teach our young that they would be better off not making waves. *Make sure you enjoy the water and make waves.*

The pain of rejection is like the vaccination the doctor gave you to prevent a certain illness. If you had avoided the temporary pain of the shot, the consequences could have been devastating. But by overcoming your reservations about a little pain then, you became immune to the disease. *Any time you are hesitant about doing anything new due to your fear of rejection, look at it as an inoculation against the "disease" of complacency.* In other words, *TAKE YOUR SHOT and GO FOR IT!*

"You can do amazing things if you have strong faith, deep desire, and just hang in there."
Norman Vincent Peale

E

Chapter 4

EXCEPTIONS TO THE RULE
The Fourth Secret of the NO REJECTION Process

"The reward is equal to the contribution."
Author Unknown

Miserable, Miserable – What's the Worst Rejection?

There will always be rejection in your life. After applying the ideas in this book, you'll find that almost all rejection is healthy for your growth. While that may seem incredible, there is only one type of rejection that really causes misery – the rejection we give ourselves.

Since this rejection is self-inflicted, it creates a special kind of misery. We are its primary cause, and we alone can cure it. Rejecting ourselves for something we did or didn't do often causes us to wallow in self-pity and guilt. If we let our self-blame grow from this one instance and generalize our feelings, they could blossom into the belief that we alone are the cause of many of the world's problems. From here we are likely to dwell on what we are not going to do any more. This equates to nothing left to do but stay away from new things and fresh ideas. Even at this early stage, you can probably surmise the result of this attitude. It would be like a caterpillar not believing it will sprout wings and fly, crawling back into its cocoon and never coming out.

What's really puzzling is how simple these self-rejections are to recognize and yet how few people seem to notice them. Once you see them for what they are, you can rid yourself of these dark clouds hanging over your life. As you gain a full understanding of how to identify your self-rejections, you can prevent them from ever again interfering with your life.

The challenge is in recognizing the self-rejection in the first place. Many times it's like the flu; masked behind symptoms, it can go undetected until it's in full force. It's important to learn to recognize and identify the symptoms and realize they are the seeds of self-rejection. Symptom recognition can speed the cure and quicken your recovery. You can then grow into the person you are destined to be, and live the life you want.

What are these Symptoms?

Dr. James R. Sherman identified some of these symptoms in his book *REJECTION – How to Survive Rejection and Promote Acceptance.* He refers to them as self-inflicted wounds. Here they are:

Self-Abandonment. You've given up on yourself. And since you were feeling abandoned when you were rejected, you now embrace abandonment as a way of life.

Self-Abuse. If you now hate yourself for seeking approval in the first place, you begin to abuse yourself in excess. You overwork your body, drink to excess, or practice other forms of self-inflicted abuse to punish yourself for doing something you now feel is stupid.

Self-Accusation. You blame yourself for every aspect of the rejection. It's obvious to you that only those who are wrong and at fault are rejected. If this were a crime, you would plead guilty.

Self-Annihilation. You have convinced yourself you have no value. You believe you have no control over your life and the failures you experience are controlled by destiny.

Self-Betrayal. Because of rejection, you feel that by revealing your true feelings, you have betrayed your own confidence.

Self-Condemnation. After a slanted analysis of the rejection, you've come to the conclusion that you are, without question, guilty of unpardonable acts. This is the reason for total rejection. You tell everyone close to you with the hope that they'll punish you even more.

Self-Criticism. After being rejected, all you do is focus on your faults and shortcomings. The more you dwell on rejection, the more self-critical you become.

Self-Deception. Because you believe you are unable to accept the fact that you have been rejected, you begin to act with qualities you just don't have. You become a hypocrite just to be accepted.

Self-Defeat. You perceive that since you have been rejected in the past, you anticipate rejection with everything new you try. You become a self-fulfilling prophecy and those you want acceptance from continue to reject you.

Self-Denial. Due to your guilt from rejection, you've convinced yourself that you should have never sought acceptance in the first place. You won't even allow yourself to be happy.

Self-Despair. You feel so hopeless that you never expect to feel good or be successful again. Your confidence dwindles to nothing and your incentive to keep going disappears.

Self-destruction. You seriously look at suicide as the get even alternative. It is your way of getting back at the person who rejected you.

Self-Doubt. Your rejection has caused you to lose faith in your own abilities to gain acceptance. Everything you do is filled with feelings of not expecting much.

Self-Effacement. Your desire to be noticed has become a thing of the past and now your only desire is to become part of the unnoticed background. If there is any possibility of being rejected, you shrink further into the corner.

Self-Humiliation. You can't believe you were stupid enough to think something you did or thought of could be accepted. Your self-respect is either gone or blocked out and your self-esteem is only a distant memory.

Self-Justification. First you review all the reasons why you were seeking acceptance. Then you spend the rest of your time justifying any of your shortcomings that caused your rejection.

Self-Pity. You make a career out of dwelling on the misery of your rejection. The more you do it, the better it *seems* to feel – seems is the key word. Soon the real feelings are interchangeable with the imaginary.

Self-Punishment. Only after abusing yourself in any way possible, or taking dangerous physical risks, do you feel that the price of your rejection has been paid. You believe you need to be punished for trying something new.

Self-Renunciation. Due to rejection you've decided to give up all your dreams, goals, and desires. You would rather not have them, than face further rejection.

Self-Repression. Because of past rejections you begin to fear the future. Consequently, you keep all thoughts and dreams to yourself to avoid new rejections. You try nothing new to avoid the risk of being rejected again.

Self-Righteousness. Your focus becomes so narrow you're convinced that it's them and not you who are wrong. It could get to the point where your rejectors become evil incarnate and you're a martyr.

We need to recognize the symptoms of self-rejection so we can treat the disease. Such rejection can lead to a negative life change if it is left to grow and fester. The good news is that the antidote is the disease itself. You can actually use the self-rejection as an immune system builder by getting an "injection" of it, then growing through it! In chapter 16 we explore self-rejection further.

Some Rejection Can Be Controlled or Eliminated

You could be rejected because of your appearance. I'm not speaking of a disfigurement due to birth or accident. Nor am I speaking about the color of your skin, shape of your eyes, or texture of your hair. People who reject you based on those things are not discussed in this book. (I will include them should I ever do a book on ignorance.) I am speaking of a more superficial nature. Here's an analogy to help you understand.

In addition to writing, I conduct training and motivational seminars. Part of making those seminars a success, which is how I earn a living, is to appear at the client's place of business to sell them on the advantages of having their people attend. Understand that many years of knowledge and actual experience are locked up inside me. In my field I am even considered an "expert" by some. But, let me ask you this. If I were to appear at your office door wearing jeans and a sweatshirt, would you be more or less likely to hire me?

While I agree that clothes do not make the person, I can tell you that what you wear will often determine whether or not your good qualities will ever be discovered. The other side of the coin is, suppose you want me to treat *you* as the important person you believe you are. Would it be unreasonable for me to expect you to take the time to dress like you thought *I* was important enough for you to get my attention?

Grooming and cleanliness are other big areas you can utilize to promote acceptance of you and your ideas. Men need to be clean shaven, preferably with no facial hair. Have you noticed how company presidents and other successful male leaders are usually clean shaven?

Hair needs to be neat and clean – avoid waterfall haircuts or the skinhead look. They just aren't attractive to most people. Needless to say, everyone needs to shower or bathe daily, if not for themselves, then out of respect for others. Also, be sure to use deodorants and apply cologne or perfume sparingly.

Finally, earrings look great on women, but not on men. Also, women need to be aware of the length of their dresses and skirts in order to project a businesslike appearance. Ladies also need to wear tops with a conservative neckline. Any jewelry women wear needs to be in keeping with a professional appearance (no enormous dangle earrings).

Bring Out the Best In Yourself and Others

During my career I have interviewed hundreds of people who applied for sales positions. Yet, I have never been able to predict, just by looking at someone, whether or not they'd be successful once they were hired. If they showed up for an interview without taking the time to look at what their clothes and outward appearance said to me, we never even talked. Unfortunately, I may have let some talent slip away.

The challenge was they didn't realize they had any talent. Now I *look at people not as they are, but as they can be.* Afterall, everybody has to start somewhere. The key is we all need someone who believes in us.

Bring out the best in yourself by GROOMING AND DRESSING LIKE YOU MEAN IT! If you really want to work for or associate with someone or have them want to work for or associate with you, show them respect by the way you dress and groom yourself. Make a lasting positive impression. Reduce the possibility of rejection. Look the part as much as you can.

Many times I have talked to people who were uncomfortable wearing suits and ties. But they were so determined to reach their goals, they were willing to do whatever it took. In any endeavor that means you need to get out of your "comfort zone" or "familiar zone." Excellent grooming and dressing your best and knowing it, gives you a sense of accomplishment. This boosts your confidence and self-esteem. In most cases, the high paying opportunities go to those with these two key qualities.

Rejection Based On Lack Of Understanding

Here's another type of rejection within your control. When I first moved to New England, I sensed a strong tie with tradition. As I became more accustomed to the people, I began to observe how that tradition continued. When I was explaining a financial aspect with someone older from this area, I would often use a computer. There were many people who, at that time, didn't see much use for a computer and in some cases actually feared them. Their fears generally stemmed from a lack of understanding of how computers gave the answers so quickly.

When a true tradition-oriented New Englander could not see how I got an answer, they assumed I may have had something to hide. Other times they just didn't understand what I did. In either case, their pride often got the best of them. Rather than face the fear of embarrassment, they would simply reject the idea.

The mistake I often made was that I would defend the idea based on its own merits, only to be rejected more firmly. Once I learned to make sure the concept was understood prior to asking for acceptance, it dramatically reduced the number of rejections. The only rejections left were all based on the merits of the concept.

Every time we venture out to discover if an idea will be accepted, we first need to make sure all parties involved understand the concept. If you don't do this, you'll probably never be sure why your idea was rejected.

When you spend the time and energy to make sure the concept is understood, you may gain new insights about how to improve it. You may then realize more acceptance, or even decide to abandon it for other pursuits. All of these results cause growth.

Rejection Caused By What You Fear Others May Think, Say, or Do

The last type of rejection we'll consider in this chapter is challenging to discover. But as with all challenging discoveries, there are greater benefits. I'm speaking of the rejection that is given to your idea as a result of the givers' own fear of rejection from their peers.

Consider politics.   How often have we heard of Congressional bills that had support behind closed doors, but when they entered the legislative chambers, the pressures from others caused a shift in votes? Well, that's just politics, you may say. What would you expect?

How about you? Did you ever change your mind because of the change in the polls? Did you ever root for a team *after* they began winning? If so, it's likely you have rejected something based solely on your own fear of being rejected by others.

Now you're asking yourself, where are the big benefits in all of this? Stay with me for a moment and I'll show you.

Let's say you discover a person who would reject an idea of yours only because of their own fear of rejection by their peers. Say you presented your concept and got rejected. You then defended your stand by pointing out a weakness in the person you were looking to for acceptance. How successful do you think you would you be? How likely are they to be open-minded when you approach them with another concept?

Accept Others Unconditionally

What if you started accepting others unconditionally, regardless of how they react to your plan? What if you said to them upfront that whatever they decide is best for them is fine with you too? You just wanted to share an opportunity with them. What if this course of action lets them decide they could be accepted by someone, regardless of which choice they made? If they reject you and your idea, they are accepted by their peers. If they accept you and your idea, it will be on the value of your plan because they already have *your* acceptance. You have placed them in a true win-win situation where they can decide what's truly best for them. What does that tell them about you? Now how do you think they will react to future ideas you may present to them?

Let's look at the big picture. When you simply accept them regardless of their decision, here's what the benefits will be:

◆ Your idea stands on its own merit. This is the best you can hope for.

You have created an opportunity for someone to learn independence. That makes you a great teacher and the greatest way to learn is to teach.

Because of your acceptance, someone you have come in contact with now has more strength to deal with rejection.

Since they are open mined, they may be able to make suggestions to improve your idea.

Preventing rejection for the "wrong" (non-value) reasons lets your ideas stand on their own merit. They will either be accepted and benefit others, or rejected. Then you can move on. Preventing the "wrong" kind of rejection saves time for all concerned.

Here's some key points to remember:

Learn to recognize and eliminate self-rejection. If you really want something – show it by how you present yourself. Dress and groom yourself so your appearance works strongly for you instead of against you.

Before you ask someone to accept or reject an idea, do everything in your power to make sure they understand the concept. When you have done everything you can and they either still don't understand it, or choose not to accept it, go share it with someone else. Use the rejection as a learning experience and motivation to move-on.

Accept everyone unconditionally for who they are. This takes the fear of rejection away from them (and you) before presenting anything to them for acceptance. This will help keep both parties at ease.

Oftentimes, when someone rejects your idea or proposal, it may mean that they are just headed in a different direction. They have their own agenda or their "plate" may already be too full – at the moment. Approach them later about it and they may say, "OK I'm ready now."

J

Chapter 5

JUST SUPPOSE....

The Fifth Step of the NO REJECTION Process

"Whether you believe you can or believe you can't... you're right."
Henry Ford

On the Spur of the Moment – I've Made a Decision

That's it! I've decided to go out on my own to give seminars and do consulting. I will work hard at providing a wealth of information and strive to give all my clients more than they paid for. I will be paid extremely well and will be able to retire 20 years earlier and spend time with my family. That's it – that's my goal.

The Paralysis of Analysis

Instead of making a positive action decision, just suppose you analyze such an opportunity to death by looking at everything negatively.   You might ask yourself these questions...

 ♦ Just suppose I'm not getting into the "right" business?
 ♦ Just suppose I don't have the "right" marketing plan?
 ♦ Just suppose there's a recession?
 ♦ Just suppose traveling around the country gets boring?
 ♦ Just suppose people don't pay on time?
 ♦ Just suppose I don't sell out at my seminars?
 ♦ Just suppose people don't think I'm smart?
 ♦ Just suppose my relatives give me a hard time about leaving my family?
 ♦ Just suppose I make more money and can't handle the taxes?
 ♦ Just suppose the people who can't get in my seminars get angry with me?
 ♦ Just suppose someone copies my idea and does it less expensively?

These are all things you need to consider, right? After all, you can't be too careful now, can you? Or can you? Have you ever heard of the "paralysis of analysis"? Limiting risk is one thing, but creating rejection by using risk as an excuse is another.

Just Suppose We Used "Just Suppose" in a Positive Light?

 ♦ Just suppose I focus on nothing else!
 ♦ Just suppose I have a positive affect on everyone who attends my seminars?
 ♦ Just suppose I am responsible for inspiring and helping others succeed?
 ♦ Just suppose we keep needing bigger and bigger rooms to hold all the people?

- Just suppose my relatives watch out for my family so that I can succeed?
- Just suppose I visit a different part of the country every week?
- Just suppose business gets so good it creates more customers?
- Just suppose people think I'm brilliant?
- Just suppose so many people emulate me that I become the industry leader?

Imagine trying to reject someone who is focusing on positive questions like these. It would be almost impossible. Someone who is this focused on positive outcomes is bound to succeed. They see nothing else but success for themselves and their idea.

Your mind always provides answers for your questions. When you ask the appropriate questions you get the appropriate answers. If you don't like the answers you're getting, maybe you need to be asking different questions!

Using "just suppose" (in a positive light) is basically a "kit" for building dreams. Take another look at the last series of questions and you'll see a dream being built. Now consider an action you've been wanting to take and substitute your own words to follow "just suppose." See what a powerful dream you can build for yourself. Before you cast this off as some kind of psychobabble, ask yourself one thing – Just suppose this works?

Picture Your Dreams – Dreambuild
Make a list of things you would like to do or have. This is a part of *dreambuilding* Maybe you want your own business. Maybe you'd like to spend more time with your family and travel. Perhaps a new car, a boat, a house on the water, or

season tickets for your favorite team's games excites you. Whatever it is you want, picture yourself having it. You may not have it immediately, but when you dreambuild, you'll start heading for your dream. As Dr. David Schwartz says in *The Magic of Thinking Success,* "A great life begins with a great dream." Now begin the "just suppose" process.

Don't worry if the "just supposes" come out negative; let them. Before you can cure something, you need to know what you're dealing with before you determine what action to take. In this case, you need to empty the negatives out of your mind. Once you have completed the negative part of your list, put it away. Go do something positive, no matter what it is. Just do something nice for either somebody else or yourself that uplifts you. Take the kids to the movies, buy your spouse a small gift, make a donation to charity, read a positive book, or listen to a motivational tape.

Now get yourself ready to *dreambuild.* Go get some things that show what you want. A picture of your dream house, a car or a vacation brochure, or some other things that show your dreams could really light your fire.

Grab your list and the pictures of what you want. Each time you read one of your negative "just supposes" look at those pictures. Immediately write down a positive "just suppose" that is exactly the opposite of your negative one. For example, "Just suppose all my friends get jealous of my mink coat?" After looking at the picture, you could write: "Just suppose I told them how they could get one too. I'll bet that would brighten their day and everyone would be thrilled." Then quickly, with a thick marker, cross out the negative "just suppose."

Once you've completed this process with every negative, you've laid a strong foundation for a rejection-proof dreambuild. Now each night before you go to bed, read the positive "just supposes" out loud. Read them again each morning to give you the reason, energy, and motivation to start your day. This'll help keep you in a positive frame of mind. You'll also attract other positive people to you who'll help protect you from rejection's potential negative effects.

Run Toward Your Dream

Proper use of "just suppose," will help keep you headed in the right direction. Negative "just supposes" cause you to run away from things, which puts distance between you and others. Positive "just supposes" keep you running toward your dream. Any time you are running toward something, it doesn't matter what happens along the way. You can overcome any obstacles. The important thing is you are always getting closer to your objective. As long as what you're striving for keeps getting closer, your belief will go up and you'll feel it is more realistic and attainable. Your energy and determination will increase. The obstacles of rejection won't seem as large, the setbacks not as painful, and the delays not as long.

Because of my business, I get to meet many successful people, including millionaires. In all of the seminars where I've listened to these millionaires answer questions, one question has never come up. No one has ever asked them how long it took them to become wealthy. Why? Because it really doesn't matter. No one's in competition with anyone except themselves.

Learn a lesson from a millionaire. Keep driving toward your dream, blasting through the rejection along the way. You will make it and those that come to congratulate you won't be concerned about how long it took you. There are great friendships to be found in your quest for success and true friends will always encourage and be patient with each other.

Chapter 6

EVERYBODY'S DOING IT
The Sixth Secret of the NO REJECTION Process

"My interest is in the future because I am going to spend the rest of my life there."

Charles F. Kettering

Do You Want To Be Average?

So many people go through life just wanting to fit in and be average. I refuse to believe anyone is born to this plight. Ask any kid what they want to be. I challenge you to find just one who says they are really looking forward to being average! Most of them all start out dreaming of becoming a famous athlete, doctor, firefighter, astronaut, or the like. As we become adults, what causes us to transition away from dreaming great dreams? And more importantly, can it be changed?

First, let's look at where you find average people. You can travel the world and meet them at every corner and in between. They are the majority. How did they get that way if most of them once had dreams and ambitions? As these kids grew older they entered into what I call the "MAKE-A-

LIVING" Training Program. Each has been "trained" by society, the media, advertisers, and governments that *this is as good as it is going to get*. They say the only way to live is to get a good job; provide for the next generation so they can have it better than you; and let it go at that.

Better, How?

The next generation will probably have many of their bigger dreams destroyed as well. They'll just get other jobs, and provide for the next generation. Are we evolving into a race of mostly average beings controlled by outside influences? Are we becoming like sheep, destined to follow the crowd? Are we convinced that since the human body consists of only a few dollars worth of chemical compounds, that's all we're worth?

Why Are We So Valuable?

I, for one, enjoy considering what our true value is. One of the things that makes us human is our incredible mind. To duplicate all of its functions you'd need a computer the size of the World Trade Center which would cost billions. Yet, with all that artificial intelligence, there's still one thing a computer cannot do. It can't generate a single new thought on its own! What does that make you worth?

My son and I enjoy collecting sports cards. One thing that adds to the value of a card is its rarity. For example, a 1912 Honus Wagner card once sold at auction for well over $400,000! There are 12 of them known to exist in the world today. Everything I have learned tells me we humans are rarer than that. We are "one-of-a-kind" original articles! What's something that rare worth?

Self-Esteem

Most people know the price of things, but in many cases, they don't know the value. You need to understand that your value in the eyes of the world begins with *the respect you feel for yourself*– your self-esteem.

Your self-esteem can be eroded only by value judging and comparison. Whenever you put someone else on a pedestal and think they are better than you, you automatically put yourself down. That causes you to *feel* less respect for yourself. It then becomes difficult, if not impossible, for you to approach that person and present your idea, product, or service to them. As Dale Carnegie says in *How to Win Friends and Influence People,* "Never criticize, condemn, or complain." As you apply this wisdom, remember to follow this rule as you talk to yourself too, not just others!

Remember, we're all equal in value in the eyes of God. No one is better than you and you're no worse than anyone else! We all have different skills and contributions but that doesn't mean any one of us is worth more or less because of that. Nobody is a "big deal," and anyone who thinks they are is in trouble and needs to develop some humility. Once you understand and accept this, you'll be able to approach anyone. In fact, you may want to adopt this attitude – *That person's going to be glad they met me!*

Ask Yourself Questions

Asking questions is another powerful tool for you to build your success with. Your brain is so powerful that it will do everything it can to give you an answer to any question you ask about yourself. For example, if after experiencing rejection, you find yourself asking, "Why me?" often enough, your mind will work to come up with a logical answer based on the input it has received throughout your life. Some typical answers your brain may give you could be: you weren't listening, you were acting like a jerk, and on-and-on-and-on.

If you don't like the answers you're getting to your questions, it may be that you need to change your behavior. ASK MORE QUESTIONS! What could I have done to make the situation better? Your mind has the answer. How can I be more effective in business? Let your mind tell you the answer. How could I change in order to be more successful? You just did.

Know "WHY" You're Doing Something and You'll Figure Out "How"

Many times people are average simply because they lose sight of their reasons for doing something. Zig Ziglar once told this story.

Two men were digging a ditch for a railroad company. One was young and had just started and the other was bent over from years of digging. The younger one said, "Didn't I see you getting out of the chairman's limousine last night?" The old man looked up and replied, "Yes, every so often we have dinner together." The young man was amazed that someone digging ditches had the chance to dine with the chairman of the board.

"How do you get to have dinner with him?" he asked. "Well," the old timer explained, "I've known him for years. As a matter of fact, we both started here on the same day digging ditches." "Wow!" was the reply, "And he went all the way to chairman. What happened to you?" Remorse showed in the old man as he finished the story. "You see, back when we started, he came to work for the company, and I came here for $1.30 an hour."

To me, the moral of the story is that, *WHY we do something most often determines the outcome.* Average people have often lost their *reason WHY.*

Think about this. If I asked you *how* to do your job, you could probably tell me. If you have your own business, it's likely you could tell me *how* to run it. If you are in any type of sales, you could certainly tell me *how* to sell whatever it is you sell. Assuming all of this is true, are you as successful as you could be? Are you enjoying what you do? Are you experiencing the joy and satisfaction you want? If not, why not? What is the *WHY* of what you're doing? Is it enough to keep you doing what you're doing? If not, why not? Would you do it for free?

That is precisely the reason some people you know are more successful than others. They not only know the "how," but they also understand the power of "WHY." Once you harness this power, you can change every aspect of how you see, hear, and feel about things. Once you put plans into action based on the *WHY* rather than the how, you'll be amazed at the success you will achieve. Once you decide *WHY* you are above average, your mind will begin to do something you may not have done in years – DREAM! (And I don't mean the sleep variety either.) But more than that, once you realize *why* your dreams are important to you, your mind will show you *how* to achieve them.

What's the Alternative?

Sound too good to be true? Consider the alternative. Imagine yourself five years from now, without a dream. Picture your life as if it's five years down the road and today you decided to be average. If you let your mind get a clear and honest picture of how that would be, you'll hear the questions average people ask. "Is this all there is?" "If only I had: done this, bought that, said this, tried that, and such." You fill in the blank. "What would my life be like?" You'll hear statements that average people make. "It just wasn't meant to be." "That's life." "You can't fight city hall." "Just go with the flow." (Even a *dead* fish floats down stream!) Some people use "go with the flow" to mean "be accepting."   Here we're talking about complacency. Kathleen Casey Theisen clarifies acceptance, which some people misinterpret as complacency – "Acceptance is not submission; it is acknowledgment of the facts of a situation. Then deciding what you're going to do about it."

What would be different if today you decided being average simply isn't good enough? Now let's look five years down the road. What does your mind say now? "I'm glad I did that." "I can hardly believe these exciting things have happened." "My dream came true!"

Listen to your kids (Or, if you aren't a parent, listen to children who admire, love, and respect you). How would it feel to have them think of you as a hero? If you know that's how it could be, is there really any alternative? The *Bible* says, "Seek and you shall find." Are you looking for an excuse not to do something or are you looking for reasons to do something? Either way you'll get your answer.

Here's a Few Ideas That may Help Your Thinking:
If you find yourself saying this... Say this instead:

I tried that once....	I'll get it right.
Why me?	Why not me?
I can't.	I need to....
I have no choice.	I'll find a better way.
What's in it for me?	I'd be happy to do it.
Everybody's doing it.	I do it because it's right.
I don't have time.	Busy people get it done.
What do you want from me?	What can I do for you?
These things happen.	I control my destiny.

Make Excuses and You Lose

You have the power within yourself to overcome the plight of being average in any area of your life where you want to excel. The tiniest thing you can do that is beyond what average people do is all it takes to break through mediocrity. The only thing that can prevent this from happening is if you make excuses. As Benjamin Franklin once said, "He who is good at making excuses is seldom good at anything else."

If you believe you need excuses to get through life, save yourself some time and aggravation. Find an excuse you really like and stick with it. For example: A guy goes next door to borrow a lawnmower. His neighbor looks at him and says "no." When asked "Why?" he replied, "I need it to wash the car." The guy was a bit puzzled and asked, "Why do you need the mower to wash the car?" The reply, " Since I don't want to lend you my mower, one excuse is as good as another!"

Remember, an excuse is a thin shell of truth stuffed with a lie! The dictionary defines an excuse as a cover-up, a lie, a ruse. Make excuses and you lose. Tell the truth and you win.

Is Average OK?

What's wrong with being average? After all, average people usually don't harm anyone; they keep to themselves, and mind their own business. What's wrong with that? Actually, nothing. However, by being average you probably won't live the kind of life you want, nor make much of a difference in the world.

Somewhere near you is the greatest source of natural resources the world has ever known. Visit there before you read another chapter of this book. It doesn't matter where you are. There is such a place just minutes from you – your local cemetery. In its ground are some of the greatest ideas that will *never* be shared. It holds inventions that will *never* improve the quality of life and art that will *never* be viewed.

It keeps music that will *never* be heard, and future generations that will *never* be born.

Cemeteries are filled mostly with people who just wanted to fit in. They went with the flow, and faded into obscurity without contributing much. You can almost hear them saying, "What difference could I have made? I'm only one person." As Thoreau said, "Most men lead lives of quiet desperation." Do you want to be one of them?

How Do You Rise Above Being Average?

Average people believe that things just happen *to* them. The reality is that *what happens to us happens for us* so we can grow and become what we were created to be. Furthermore, we were also given free will so we can control our own destiny!

I could give you a long drawn out explanation, but the fact is, you already have risen above average. You see, change doesn't take place at the end of the transformation. It begins the instant you *commit* to making the change. Your *desire* to rise above average made it so. As soon as you decided to change, you began! As Robert H. Schuller says, "Beginning is half done." This is a tremendous success since the majority of people don't even ask how they can be anything but average. And most of the people who do ask, quickly come up with excuses not to pursue their destiny.

You are to be commended for deciding to be above average and taking action. (Just the fact that you're reading this book shows you've made a decision and are moving-on.) You can feel great that your efforts will make a positive difference in the world. I know that might sound a bit like "pie-in-the-sky" but, in a year's time you could help 4,000 people just by making a difference in the lives of twelve!

Let's say you helped one person a month become focused on the success they could have. As repayment, you asked only that they begin doing the same for others. If you go through the numbers, you'll find that you will have impacted the lives of 4,096 people in just one year! Later I'll share how I got that number. Replace any thoughts of your insignificance with this idea. If you still have any doubts, ask yourself this question. How many lives did Jesus Christ change by making a difference in the lives of 12? And remember, they were just "average" fishermen when He met them.

Here's Some Food for Thought

1) What is one thing you have been afraid to do because of others?_____

_____

_____

Remember this. If what you are thinking of doing causes you to fear what others may think – congratulations, you're on the right track. As John L. Mason says in *An Enemy Called Average,* "Ingratitude and criticism are going to come; they are a part of the price paid for leaping past mediocrity." Furthermore, *as long as you do what's right for you and it's not hurting others, it's right for them too!* They may not understand it when you begin, but time will prove it so!

2) Within the next 24 hours take one step towards doing what you fear. Start by asking yourself some questions: How will this help others? Will it inspire them to overcome their own fears? Will it serve as an example to my children or others I care about? What

have I got to WIN? What are the alternatives to not doing it? Would I be happy with these alternatives in the long run?

3) How are you feeling now that you have taken that step?_____

_____

_____

"Not doing more than average is what keeps the average down."
Charlie "Tremendous" Jones

".....you can accept fear as a fact of life rather than a barrier to success."
Susan Jeffers, Ph.D.

"An indecisive person allows instability to creep into every area of his life. If we don't decide what is important in our own lives, we will probably end up doing only the things that are important to others."
John L. Mason

C

Chapter 7

CONFIDENCE, FEAR, LOVE, & SELF-ESTEEM

The Seventh Secret of the NO REJECTION Process

"Change is inevitable, growth is optional."
Author Unknown

Rejection Is a Part of Life

It's probably safe to say you now realize rejection, just like acceptance, success, failure, happiness, and sadness, is a part of life. All these things contribute to your personal development and personal history; thus making you unique. What determines where you go in life is how you respond to and work with these ingredients.

How serious are you to find out what causes you to respond in certain ways? How can you get to the bottom of what's holding you back? How can you "break through" your old ways of thinking that aren't serving you anymore?

You want to gain a greater understanding so you can learn to better accept rejection for what it is – a part of life, here to stay. You also want to learn how to respond to it so it is beneficial to you.

We all know that a cake usually consists of sugar, flour, eggs, salt, and other ingredients. If, however, you're not careful with the proportions, I doubt your guests will be asking for more dessert! The ingredients need to be blended in exact proportions to achieve the desired result. If you're haphazard in measuring, I hope you don't care about the outcome. If you are expecting a great tasting cake, you'll probably be disappointed. If you add more salt and use less sugar, the end result is more likely to resemble bread.

Some Of the Essential Ingredients for Success
The proper "ingredients" are also essential for success. We are all born with intact self-esteem, but others usually come along, "beat-us-up" mentally and damage it. Different factors can hurt our self-esteem, as well as affect our fears, confidence, and ability to give and receive love. The great thing is, once we become aware of what's really going on in our lives, we can change it. The best way to make this happen is to have a mentor – someone who will take you under their wing and coach you to success.

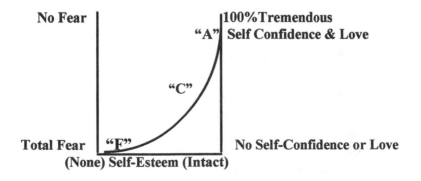

How Do These Ingredients Affect Each Other?

This diagram represents how some of the essential success ingredients relate. Notice that as our self-esteem heals, our fear of rejection goes down, while our self-confidence and ability to love go up. This is important.

Some people have been so negatively affected by rejection, that it severely impacts all or many areas of their life. Generally speaking, the areas most affected are love and self-esteem. As your self-esteem is damaged, your capacity to love diminishes. As your self-confidence shrinks and you become more concerned what others think, say, or do, your self-esteem and ability to love decline, and your fears are magnified. This could be represented by point "F." The person at this point is near failure; they're unsuccessful, unfulfilled, unhappy, and angry.

Have you ever known someone who is successful at almost everything they do? You have always admired how they seem to know which risks are worth taking and which need to be avoided. They have a wonderful marriage and people just like to be around them. That person is at or near point "A." They're successful, happy, and living a fulfilling life.

The person at point "C" is average; they have mediocre success. Sometimes they're happy, but more often they're not. They're not really fulfilled or living the life they want. These people might say they're doing "OK"!

The good news is, anybody who chooses can be a point "A." The key to it all is self-esteem. The more intact yours is, the more success, happiness, and fulfillment you'll have; no fear can stop you.

Anyone with intact self-esteem and a great capacity to love can keep their fear of rejection in check and reduce it while exploring new opportunities. If this fear is allowed to expand, something has to give; usually it's our self-esteem and self-confidence.   When our fear of doing something grows, our confidence in doing it diminishes.   We may even begin to feel inadequate about our ability to do other tasks as well.

When we stretch and do new things, our confidence grows and our self-esteem gets repaired.   Our increased strength overpowers our fear and makes it less likely that we'll allow our fear to stop us.   *The more intact your self esteem is, the less you fear rejection.*   With totally intact self-esteem, rejection will roll off you like water off a duck's back!

Exercise Your Mind and Associate With Positive People

To be effective in dealing with rejection, you need a continuing program of mental growth and association with positive people.   You can't go to the gym, get the workout of a lifetime one morning, and then be healthy forever.   Shorter workouts, three or four times a week, along with a balanced, healthy diet can help keep you in peak condition.

The same holds true for your mental health.   You can "exercise" all you want but if you feed your mind nothing but mental "junk" food, you'll never move-on.   A sure way to fail is letting yourself be ruled by the "committee of they." Listening to people who either don't care or don't want you to succeed doesn't work.   Yielding to that inner voice of fear telling you to avoid rejection also guarantees failure.

Watching television can negatively affect you.   Negative news, violence, and non-educational shows can turn your mind into mush.   It can also be detrimental to read the newspaper, which seldom portrays the bright side of life. Successful people fill their minds with "personal growth" food rather than "junk" food.

When you follow the suggestions offered here, you'll be able to use rejection as a "vaccination" against failure. Periodic doses of rejection accelerate your growth and strengthen your mental well-being. *The more rejection you get, the more successful you'll be!*

Keep a "Success Notebook"

Keep a "Success Notebook" to help yourself stay motivated. Write in it every success you encounter every day. List separately, on another page, any rejection and *apparent* setback. Once you recognize the signals that tell you you're not on-track, you'll change direction. The path you were taking may not have been leading you toward your desired destination. Remember, what happens to you happens for you. Thomas Edison best illustrates this point. When he was asked why he kept going on his quest to invent the light bulb after 999 failures he replied, "I have not failed. I have simply discovered 999 different ways not to invent the electric light."

Also enter the discoveries you make from your successes in your notebook, and be very detailed. Describe how you *felt*. What was going through your mind? Jot down whatever you can recall about your success. When you feel you aren't having a particularly great day, look at your list of successes and "flex" your self-esteem and self-confidence. Remind yourself that you *feel* respect for yourself. Tell yourself you're a successful person who has just discovered a new way to have a great day. Focus on the positive, so circumstances won't matter. As Snowden McFall says in her book *Fired Up!,* " Every time I feel like I'm not getting anywhere on my dream, I remember to do my daily success list... my whole attitude shifts and I am 'Fired Up!' about what I've done. You can get 'Fired Up!' too."

Act "As If " and Be Specific

If you're not at the point where you *feel* the self-respect and self-confidence to carry yourself as a success, consider modeling someone. Find someone you admire and duplicate what you admire. As the saying goes, Act "as if." Until you understand yourself better, and figure out what you need to do, model yourself after that person. Until you create your own success habits, continue modeling yourself after someone you believe is successful and do what they do. If you discover they aren't really the kind of person you thought they were, that's OK. Realizing that and changing role models is a success in itself. Keep "fine-tuning" and you'll eventually get it.

Get specific. When bodybuilders prepare for a contest they often concentrate on specific areas of weakness in order to improve. You won't make much progress being vague; get down to the details of what skills *you* need to improve.

Reap the Benefits of How You Affect and Help Others

If you believe you'll never be able to make a difference and give up, you'll miss the opportunity to help someone else. Remember *one of life's great serendipities is that it's impossible to help someone without helping yourself.* When you're being supportive to someone else, helping them improve an aspect of their life, you automatically help yourself!

What you do affects others. When you have a great attitude, it is impossible for it not to affect some of the people you come in contact with.

In some cases they may be in a mental fog where they don't appear to be affected or they may choose to stay entrenched in their own negativity. All you can do is be the best you that you know how to be. The rest is up to them. (Their behavior is their responsibility; it's a reflection of their own thinking and feelings.) Conversely, if you are miserable you could bring down the attitudes of a room full of people (if they let you). When you understand that you create your attitude, you can take steps to control it. You can choose to be a negative influence that is likely to bring others down or encourage others and lift them up. Lifting them up is much more fun!

"You can have everything in life you want, if you will just help enough other people get what they want."
Zig Ziglar

"Maturity begins to grow when you can sense your concern for others outweighing your concern for yourself."
John MacNaughton

"In about the same degree as you are helpful, you will be happy."
Karl Reiland

T

Chapter 8

TURNING REJECTION INTO MOTIVATION

The Eighth Secret of the NO REJECTION Process

"When the going gets tough, the tough get going."
Frank Leahy

How Can You Be Motivated By Rejection?

A few years ago, after I submitted a manuscript for publication and received a bunch of rejection letters, I was about to give up. Postage and printing costs were eating me alive. By the time the book would have come out any monies earned would have only let me break-even. I was under the impression that writing sold on merit alone. Since up to that point, no publisher had told me anything different in their expecting a *different* result! That was until I received one of the greatest rejections of my life.

This rejection letter helped turn a dream into a profitable reality. It started off by explaining that the writing was tight (I found out later that this is a good thing), the information was well organized, and the subject had broad appeal. The next line took me to new heights until I finished it and "crashed." It said they were all set to offer me a contract. But after realizing how many similar books were already on the market, they decided it wouldn't be profitable to publish it. Let me tell you I had one heck of a pity party but nobody showed up!

What did the publisher know about my subject anyway? I had read all those books and none were as accurate as mine. They were all written by people who researched the subject years ago. I lived what I wrote. Not only was it firsthand knowledge, but it also reflected current conditions that people needed to know. If that publisher knew what I did, they would be begging for my manuscript. If they only knew how much better my information was. I would have been doing book signings instead of trying to figure out how to teach them a lesson. I asked myself, "If they're so smart, how come they didn't know this stuff?"

What Was Missing?

It's quite humbling when your answer hits you right between the eyes. They didn't know because the "expert" didn't tell them. It wasn't their responsibility to figure it out. Since these facts weren't presented to them, they had no choice but to assume it was just another book on the same subject. Why would they publish something for a small piece of the pie? Every publisher wants to capture the whole market or at least be first.

I was relieved my writing quality wasn't being rejected. It was my lack of understanding of the elements involved in *marketing* a book. I actually called this publisher, thanked them, and asked that they reconsider when the new information arrived. They explained that their window of opportunity was closed. They had all the titles they could possibly publish. Another lesson! Sometimes even when you cover all the bases, something beyond your control happens to hold you back. But it's only temporary.

Undaunted, I sent my manuscript to other publishers. It was loaded with the information they needed to make an informed decision. I told them my book was up-to-date and written from practical experience, rather than from research.

The Magical Phone Call

You probably think I'm now on easy street. Well, I sent the manuscript to about 20 more publishers and got turned down every time. Feeling rejected and dejected, I asked myself, what was I doing wrong now?

Curiosity got the better of me; I picked a publisher at random and gave them a call. As it turned out, they switched me to the same editor who had already rejected my idea. I thought about reaching through the phone and lashing out at the man. He obviously didn't know good writing when he saw it, and had no appreciation for originality. Thank God, I chickened out. I asked him what I was doing wrong. He told me. Everyone who read the book liked it. They just couldn't figure out how to promote it, so they rejected the project.

Now I know why God gave us two ears and only one mouth. By using them in that proportion, I learned I was missing a key ingredient in getting something published. Having content and quality wasn't enough. If it isn't marketable, out the door it goes! The marketability determines the final decision.   Once I understood that, I realized why they rejected it.   I had focused only on its quality and content and not its marketability.

Eventually I had a proposal that covered all the bases. My submission to the next publisher explained why the book was fresh and unique.   It discussed several ways to promote it along with my willingness to assist in any way to insure the book's success. I waited by the mailbox for what seemed like half an eternity before the answer came. It was a contract. It contained an advance.   It explained how many copies they planned to produce and how much I would make from each copy. I thought I was rejection proof.

A Surprise "Rejection"

Incredibly, the publisher went belly up (out of business) before the first copy was printed! Why do you suppose I got motivated after this? It was to my advantage. What you are now reading is the result of that rejection.

My intentions are not to teach you about the highs and lows of seeking a publisher. Just understand that even when you have covered all the bases, what you want still may not happen.   There are some things beyond your control. And even though you have something great to share, you need to determine if there's a market for it. Furthermore, even after you're ready to present it to others, you need to continue to do *whatever it takes* to make it happen. You increase your chances for success when you put all of these qualities together in a way that demonstrates your belief and commitment.

You've probably heard the expression, "What you see is what you get." Most of us think of saying it to others in our presence who are looking at us when we're talking. But also consider saying it to and about yourself when you're alone.

Using myself as an example from the previous story, here's what I mean.

Don't Take Rejection As a Personal Affront!

What if I had taken all those rejection letters personally? Do you think I would have spent more money on postage and paper to continue submitting more proposals?   If all I believed was that each letter was a personal rejection, do you think I would have been open to learning? Would I have learned I needed to tell the publisher about the uniqueness of my proposed book? Or would I have just placed their letter in my reject file for a pity party? What would you have done? If I just took these rejections as a personal affront, would I have asked enough questions to find out I needed to assist the publisher in promoting the book? Or would I have just given up? How would you have handled it? If all you're willing to believe is that you're being personally rejected, then that's what's true for you. It's just your perception. It's more likely to be a misunderstanding on your part of what other people need. It takes courage to ask questions. If you don't, you could be repeating the same behavior that caused the rejection in the first place.

I chose not to take the refusals as personal rejections. After all, it was just my first attempt at presenting a book manuscript. I may have been an expert on the subject of my manuscript, but I knew nothing about the book business. To accomplish something new, we often need to hear from others with experience that we can do it and how it needs to be done. The catch is, we need to ask questions and be humble and open to listening to others who are knowledgeable in the area we are seeking to enter.   I took this experience as a learning opportunity; therefore, I got a valuable lesson. As the saying goes, *"The teacher will arrive when the student is ready."*

Behind the Scenes of a Great Idea

All new ideas that get implemented go through a process. First, they are usually flatly rejected. Then they are consistently ridiculed. Eventually, they are accepted. Imagine constantly keeping in mind the order of how such ideas become reality. How could you not help but be motivated every time you were rejected? The stronger the rejection, the more motivated you would become. Have that attitude and you'll become flat out excited when "they" start to ridicule you. You'll know you're probably getting closer to acceptance.

Now I am *always* motivated by rejection. I know I am either onto a great idea, or I am about to learn a valuable lesson. Maintain this *attitude* whenever you present an idea, and you'll always come away with something positive whether it's accepted or rejected. You are putting yourself in a winning situation. People will respect you more and they're more likely to be open to any future ideas you may have. They may even try their best to help you improve on your ideas so that everyone gets the maximum benefit from them.

Realize there's a possibility of rejection every time you do something new or different. If you find everyone accepting what you say at face value, they may either be trying to avoid conflict or they just aren't taking you seriously. Keep looking until you find someone who will reject your idea and give you an honest reason why. They're the ones who can help you most in getting your idea ready for the world.

Rejection Is Your Friend

Another reason to get motivated by rejection is for your own good! Sometimes you get rejected simply because you deserve it. If everyone was open to or tolerant of all your ideas, you would have no rejection and no growth. How many times did you do or say something only to follow it up with questions like, "Why didn't somebody stop me"?   I would venture to say that plenty of people were prepared to stop you along the way.   You either refused to hear them or they stopped warning you after your countless refusals to listen. REJECTION IS YOUR FRIEND.

Politely listen to the warnings of those you trust who are not experts on the subject. But don't let them stop you from pursuing your idea. If you basically disagree with them, but you're not sure they're not at least partially correct, hold off on your idea until you have discussed it with a person knowledgeable about the topic. If you want to learn to fly an airplane, don't talk to your 100 year old great grandmother who has never flown. Find a CFI (Certified Flight Instructor) you can relate with and they'll tell you all about it. If, after talking with them and taking some preliminary flying lessons, it's not what you really want, fine. Whether you choose to pursue it or not, you'll be excited about the adventure of exploring the possibilities and how it expanded your horizons.

I get motivated when people I trust are challenging me on my idea. After this type of rejection, I consult with an expert. Doing this can save a tremendous amount of time and enable me to make a more informed decision. I am also able to retain the respect of others I may want to involve in projects down the road that suit them better. It also shows I respected their opinion and keeps the door open to use them as a sounding board for future ideas. While I was courteous to them, I was determined enough to follow my own direction in life and intelligent enough to search for the truth.

"The choices you make on a daily basis affect what you will have, be, or do in the tomorrow's of your life."
Zig Ziglar

I

Chapter 9

INVEST IN YOUR SUCCESS
The Ninth Secret of the NO REJECTION Process

*"I don't think much of a man who is not wiser today than he
was yesterday."*
Abraham Lincoln

Nothing Succeeds Like Success

Your success in any endeavor is based mostly on what you
put into it. So far we've dealt with the beginnings of the
success process. For most of us to be successful, we need to
make some changes. *If we are unwilling to change it is
highly likely we have already reached our maximum level of
achievement.* Now, let's take a more comprehensive look at
the process.

I use the word "success" as an acronym. It's laminated on
a business card that I look at often to remind me of the
process. Here it is.

```
Self-evaluate
Understand each task
Care
Concentrate
Expect
See
Share
```

Evaluate and Compliment Yourself

To **Self-evaluate** is essential for you to stay focused. Consider what you have accomplished every day and what adjustments, if any, need to be made for you to be on-track. Proper self-evaluation is key to maintaining confidence in your quest.   It is equally   important to review your accomplishments just as thoroughly as your setbacks. As important as it is that you evaluate a rejection, it's equally important you need to compliment yourself on an acceptance. Focusing on your "wins" helps you stay positive in the face of what appears to be your "losses."

Many of us are overly critical of ourselves and our daily performance. We may be frustrated to the extent we tend to criticize those who can help us. Be your own best friend. Be kind to yourself and others who are doing their best to support you. This makes it easier to get the help you need in order to succeed.

Remember, *never criticize, condemn, or complain. There are no statues erected to critics!* When we learn to compliment ourselves, it becomes easier to compliment others.   And just as constant criticism and lack of appreciation drives people away, sincere compliments and honest appreciation attracts them to us. When you make a mistake, look at how you can change your behavior in the future. Be equally committed to rewarding yourself with compliments as well as graciously receiving them from others when you do something well.

Focus and Gain Clarity

Understand each task you have created for yourself and how it relates to your desired outcome so you can stay on-track. Keep the destiny you have chosen for yourself clear and concise in your mind and heart. Writing it down helps to solidify it for you.   Make your dreams such an intense part of you that the details become crystal clear and alive. It is also essential that you focus on *why* you need to make your dream happen. No "ifs," "ands," or "buts" about it. Such focus and clarity are important elements to remaining on the right road (toward your dreams) during your journey. If you're not going where you want to be headed, you'll end up someplace else.

By avoiding rejection, you're taking a detour from your chosen path, because *your* path is sure to have rejection on it. You're more likely to stay on course when you have a definite route you are committed to. The funny thing is, any detour will not only take you off course, but it is likely to have rejection on it anyway! Dealing with and overcoming the rejection you are confronted with on your chosen path is like driving a car over a rough road. It's uncomfortable and noisy, but once you're over it you are still traveling in the right direction. Those few moments of discomfort are far better than the untold time that could be lost from taking a detour.

Care and Become Passionate About Your Dreams

Care about your dreams and goals. This is key. If you don't care about something, you won't pay attention to the details; the map becomes vague. That would be like driving from New Hampshire to Florida using a globe instead of a map. The lack of detail makes the journey more difficult than it needs to be. If the journey seems too difficult, some will quit and believe their dreams aren't attainable. The fact is, the way there was just too vague. *Caring is the starting point to creating passion for your goals and dreams. Your passion gives you the energy to face and overcome any obstacle more easily.* As the *Bible* says, "He did it with all his heart and prospered."

Do something with care, and the finished product will always reflect it. The quality becomes evident and people are likely to admire it. Strive for your dreams with that same kind of care, and those who associate with you are likely to become more successful as well. Lead by example. Show *them* how to care and be passionate about their dreams and goals, too. Your success is only enhanced by helping others, not by winning at any cost. Caring successfully often means others will enjoy being around you. Encourage them to become successful with you, rather than trying to prove to the world why it might be lonely at the top. For those who do find it lonely up there (because of how they arrived), tell them not to worry. They're not likely to be there very long!

Concentrate and Stay On-Track

Concentration enables you to learn what you need to know for a successful journey. By concentrating, you can learn how your actions affect your results. If necessary, you can make adjustments to get back on-track, or formulate new plans. Concentration also enables you to understand what you have learned so you can avoid repeating the same mistakes.   Concentration on your goals and dreams also helps protect you from distractions which would only slow your progress. Fear of rejection is one of those distractions. As William Matthews once said, *"The first law of success is concentration: to bend all energies to one point, and to go directly to that point, looking neither to the right nor the left."*

You need to keep your concentration on where you're going, strong in the face of fear. You need to minimize your fear so it will be easier to overcome. Concentration on the positive helps eliminate fear. To control your fear you need to focus on your dreams and goals as you take action.

Concentration enables you to deal with each rejection. Rejection itself is never the problem because it cannot grow. The *fear* of rejection is what you need to overcome. As you grow stronger you can replace your fearful thoughts with thoughts about your success. When you do this, you won't need to justify how success is not all it's cracked up to be because you'll be succeeding! Concentrate on your dreams and goals and you can overcome the *fear* of rejection.

Expect the Best

Expect to succeed when you're focused, make the necessary adjustments, and are drawn toward your dreams. *Expecting something confirms its certainty in your mind.* Begin programming yourself for the absolute attainment of your dreams and goals. Have positive expectations. When you take each step of the journey with confidence you attract others to help you. Success-oriented people will be drawn toward you. They'll want to assist you because they like being around you. You'll inspire each other to keep on achieving goals, making one dream after another come true.

As you become comfortable expecting to succeed, expect some rejection along the way. While some may think this is inviting problems, just the opposite is true. When someone lives near the water, they may build a wall to keep the water away. Building these walls doesn't invite the water to flood, but it does help the residents feel a bit more secure. They know that if there's a flood, they will be better protected. Knowing you're prepared to face rejection allows you to stay focused and move confidently toward your destination. You won't be sidetracked by the infinite combinations of "what ifs?"

Walk Backward Toward Success

See, *feel*, and *hear* your future. Begin picturing yourself as already successful. Start to *see* how you will look and what surrounds you. *Feel* how confident and happy you and your loved ones will be. *Hear* what you'll be saying to yourself and the sounds of your new environment. Ask yourself how you will act when you're successful. Once you have the answer, start acting that way now. Act "as if." How will you handle rejection once you are successful? You won't let it bother you, right? The next time you get rejected, say, "Great, I'm going the right way and getting closer to the next 'yes.'" Your future success is so real in your mind, you can easily walk backward, retracing your steps, and arrive at today.

Imagine your destination. As soon as you can experience it in your mind as if it is already happening, ask yourself this question: What did I do just before I arrived at my destination? The moment your answer becomes clear, ask yourself what you did immediately prior to that. Continue this process until you arrive back at today. I call this *walking backwards toward success*. As Stephen R. Covey, bestselling author of *The Seven Habits of Highly Effective People* says, "Begin with the end in mind." It's very powerful. Know where you are going!

Be An Encourager

Share how you became successful with others; it encourages them to succeed. To realize lasting success, you need to *share* with others what you did. When you do that, your achievement will increase in value. If you don't, your success will be empty, your achievement will be of little value, and you'll find yourself asking, "Is this all there is?"

How much value would gold have if the person who discovered it kept it to himself ? If Columbus had stayed in the New World rather than return and share his discovery, would we still believe the world is flat? His not returning would have "proved" it! It's not only the doing of great things, but also sharing of *how* you did it that's key to your success. It makes your life happier, more fulfilling, and worthwhile. It also supports others in their quest for success – inspiring them to achieve the same rewards.

Part of success comes from recognizing that we receive when we achieve and share it. If you keep your success a secret, you would have the pie crust, but not the filling. As you share with others, so they can benefit too, you are likely to be recognized and appreciated.

I am not speaking of receiving false praise. I'm talking about sincere compliments and appreciation from others because of what you've done for them. For that to occur, you need to share your success. This is not about bragging that you did this or accomplished that. That's ego-based and it turns people off.   When you're sincere in your sharing, and give other people hope, they are likely to appreciate and love you for it. Share what you did and let others know they can achieve their dreams too.

As you become successful, you need to SHARE WHAT YOU HAVE RECEIVED. This could be knowledge, money, relationships, and such. As Mark Twain once said, "Money

is like manure. It's no good unless you spread it around."
And so it is with success of any kind.

If you developed a cure for a rare disease and shared it
with those who could best benefit, wouldn't you receive
recognition? If you found and implemented a more effective
way for your company to do business, isn't it likely that
someone would acknowledge your efforts?   If it's
compliments you're after, let others benefit from your efforts
and you're likely to receive all the compliments you could
ever want.

Your Best Investment Is You

All of these things can happen when you invest in
yourself. If you aren't willing to make the investment, what
does that say about how you value yourself?   Why would
others want to invest in you if you're not taking the "risk" of
investing in yourself? The answer is, of course, obvious.
But what type of investing am I talking about? If you're not
investing at least $500 a year in your own personal
development, you're cheating yourself. Some people spend a
lot more than that.

Before you say $500 is too much money, ask yourself how
much you're worth. The nice thing is, you can do this in
"installments." At least once a month, invest in a book that
will help you reach your full potential, and read it 10-15
minutes a day. (Always keep one of these books in your
bathroom!)

Join an organization of successful people and associate
with them. Attend seminars that focus on success and satisfy
your personal development needs.

Listen to motivational and educational audiotapes every
day. Do this while you shower and get ready for work, in
your car as you travel, when you take a walk at lunch, and at

other times during the day. Use otherwise unproductive time to develop yourself.

Other things you can do for yourself that could be considered investments may not be as obvious. For instance, suppose your lawn needs mowing when you have the opportunity to move forward in your quest for success. The best thing you can do is have your child, or pay one of the neighborhood kids to mow it. This is money well spent; it's an investment. It also helps somebody else – the boy or girl you hired, who may be saving for college.

Any time you can pay to have something done so you can do something else that will improve your skills and thus your situation, that's an investment.   The key to successful investing is to generate a return. *You need to read more positive books, listen to more tapes, and attend more seminars to help you achieve your dreams as soon as possible.*   These activities accelerate your personal development. They give you the inspiration and information you need to create the positive results you want, and help you associate with others who are also moving-on.

"This one thing I do...I press on toward the mark."
The Bible, Philippians

"A strong passion for any object will ensure success, for the desire of the end will point out the means."
William Hazlitt

"It is never to late to be what you might have been."
George Eliot

O

Chapter 10

ONLY HEROES NEED APPLY
The Tenth Secret of the NO REJECTION Process

"hero(n)... Renowned for exceptional courage and fortitude."
Webster's Dictionary

What Do You Aim For?

Suppose you were looking for a new job and the title of this chapter appeared as an ad in the help wanted section. Would you apply? Most people wouldn't. The sad fact is, most people don't go for what they really want in a career. They think of their current capabilities and drop down a notch, interviewing for jobs that require less than their true ability.

Because of our fear of rejection we may set a lower standard in an attempt to reduce our risk of being rejected. Granted, when your qualifications are somewhat greater than required for the job, your chances of getting the job are better. If the job isn't offered to them, however, rejection fearing people justify it in their mind by saying the job was beneath them to begin with.

Don't just take my word for it. A top employment recruiter proved this point to me a few months ago. Understand, this person makes a living placing such people as corporate presidents and CEOs (Chief Executive Officers). When asked why there was a shortage of top level management applicants, he said it was due to the job seeker's unintact self-esteem and fear of rejection.

To prove his point, he ran newspaper ads in four major job markets – Los Angeles, New York, Dallas, and Chicago. Each ad appeared in different sections of the classifieds, had no real description of the position – just a salary, and different phone numbers to call. The first one looked like this:

WANTED
$30,000 PER YEAR
CALL (000) 555-5555

Here's the second ad:

WANTED
$300,000 PER YEAR
CALL (000)222-2222

When the week was over, a tally was done. The response to the $30,000 job ad was so great that extra operators were put on duty. Literally thousands of people called for more information.   Each city could have filled hundreds of positions from this simple ad.

Now when they tallied the total number of calls inquiring about the $300,000 job, they were equally amazed. They expected tons of calls requesting more details; but the final total, of all cities combined, was five! FIVE phone calls for the chance to earn $300,000 a year. Maybe they didn't think they would qualify. But how could they know if they didn't call?   Fear of rejection probably stopped a lot of people from calling for the higher paying job.

Want to be a hero (male or female)? Call. Until they call you back, you can tell all your friends you're considering applying for a $300,000 per year position. How would that make you feel? Maybe almost as good as if you got the job! (And maybe you'll get it.) That very *feeling* is what you want to create and enjoy. One of the objectives of this book is to help you to *feel* this way as often as possible. We want to help you repair your self-esteem so you can face rejection, be your own hero, and then a hero to others.

What's Heroic?

By looking at the definition of a hero, you'll realize that only a thin thread separates most of us from heroism. Each time you overcome an obstacle, you have done something heroic! If you are consistently practicing this kind of courage, it won't be long before people begin to admire you. Those qualities spell hero.

When you approach an obstacle or a potential rejection and keep going, and you share your experience or people notice it, you'll be an inspiration to others. Every hero I know has gone through a lot of rejection and has overcome many obstacles. Just like cowardice, heroism is a habit you choose. Whether you break through your fear of rejection or not is your choice. Setting the example for others to follow and making the more courageous choices unleashes the hero in you.

Many people don't become heroes because they fear rejection. They may believe that since they are only one person, it doesn't make any difference what they do. Do you believe what you do makes a difference? A successful businessman friend of mine talks about three types of people: Quitters, Carriers, and Builders. I can't think of a better way to evaluate yourself. Which one are you?

Quitters

I can't. It really won't make any difference. You can't fight City Hall. What's the use? Don't rock the boat. They have reached a point where the fear of rejection has become a handicap they have gotten used to. Most of the things they own are worn-out; yet they tell you they're comfortable and just broken-in. They look at the size of their paycheck instead of what they have contributed. They are generally found in large groups with fingers pointing away from themselves blaming everything on "THEM." Excuse-making is a game they excel at.

Carriers

Those who "carry" are almost as miserable as quitters; but they're not quite as far-gone. When asked to help someone succeed, they will generally pass. Yet they'll tell that person to go ahead because they can probably do it. They deny success for themselves, due to their fear of rejection; but they don't hold others back. They express a lot of heroic theory; but they have no hands-on experience.

Builders

These folks are the dreamweavers. They are focused on reaching their objectives. Everyone who comes in contact with them can benefit. They help others get what they want; thereby guaranteeing their own success. They encourage others to follow in their path, and share their pattern of success to help them achieve their dreams and goals. Builders are very patient and forgiving. They allow whatever time is needed to succeed; sometimes resetting goals as they work steadfastly and patiently with those they're helping. They are the heroes. As Henry Wadsworth Longfellow once said, "Lives of great men (people) all remind us we can make our lives sublime; and, departing, leave behind us, footprints on the sands of time."

Are You a Quitter, Carrier, or Builder?
Which one are you? Which one would you like to be? I want to be a hero. I want my children to have me as an example of setting and working towards goals. I want others to know I will do everything in my power to help them succeed. I am constantly battling with rejection and the fear it stirs up. I continue to face it, overcome it, and move-on, regardless of the challenges. I want to have a positive effect on as many people as I can. How do you want to live your life? What are your values? How many people do you think *you* can affect in a way that will enhance their lives?

Earlier in the book I introduced an idea for impacting people. So you don't have to search for it, we'll review it and go into greater detail.

Let's say you encourage one person to face rejection and go for their dreams. You agree to help them accomplish this provided they teach one other person to do the same. You commit to doing that once a month. How many people do you think you'd affect?

a. 12
b. 24
c. 144

d. 4,096

The answer is "d." Go through the numbers yourself if you wish, and you'll get the same inspiring answer. Imagine, you could have a positive impact on over 4,000 people! One person *can definitely* make a significant difference in the world.

Now let's be pessimistic. Suppose 90% of the people you have affected went back to their previous fears and habits. You would still have over 400 heroes. If we carried it out for another year, just from your initial efforts, 1,638,400 people would be affected. If 90% give up, you would still be left with 163,840 heroes after only two years of sharing.

How would you feel if you could be responsible for encouraging that kind of success? Even if you were only 1% effective with the remaining 10% in the above example, you would have made a difference in the lives of over 1,600 people. I don't know how you feel about that; but rest assured, you would never again believe one person can't make a difference.

How Can You Become a Hero?

You don't need to enter burning buildings, fight on a battlefield, discover a cure, or invent a new fuel source to be a hero. All you need to do is sincerely make a positive difference in someone's life. Don't be discouraged if the person you're trying to help doesn't get it. Make a difference anyway. Someone else may be watching and decide to follow your example. You may be a hero to someone you don't even know.

As you continue helping those you come in contact with, you will begin to feel like a hero. Be sure to remain humble though, as someone once said, "Pride comes before the fall." Once you're a humble hero in your own eyes, you can bet others will want to follow your example.

When you stop to think about it, you'll realize heroism is an inside job.   Once you have your self-esteem and self-confidence in order, you'll feel your inner strength.   It'll enable you to reach out and make a difference. You may still have fears and reservations, but they'll no longer appear as mountains that can't be climbed.   You'll realize they are opportunities in disguise.

Most heroes are unknown to the world. They live life quietly making a difference. What does it take to be a hero? Just one person who thinks you're a hero to them! With over six billion people on this planet, chances are you can make a difference for one.   That's all it takes.   When one person considers you a hero, that makes it so. Start looking for someone to help. Start doing what you know to do. Keep on helping and doing.

"It is the surmounting of difficulties that makes heroes."
Kossuth

"A hero is a man who does what he can."
Romain Rolland

"Character is the ability to carry out a good resolution long after the excitement of the moment has passed."
Cavett Robert

"When we give it all, we can live with ourselves – regardless of the results."
Zig Ziglar

Chapter 11

NICE GUYS AND GALS FINISH BEST

The Eleventh Secret of the NO REJECTION Process

"Never give in, never give in, never, never, never, never give in…."
Winston Churchill

What Does It Take To "Have It Made"?

After doing a speaking engagement, I often hang around to talk with the participants and answer questions. There's always at least one person who will let me know that I "have it made." They explain how my talk affected them and how they would love to do what I do. Then they ask what I call the "instant" question – "What do I need to do to get speaking engagements like you?"

I briefly tell them they need to get rejected and fail countless times over a 15-20 year period. They need to learn from those mistakes, and put everything they own on the line. They need to talk to large groups about their mistakes, and the lessons they learned. They need to focus entirely on helping everyone they come in contact with. They also need to have those people be better-off for having met them, and be willing to look foolish in the process.   I believe questioners use answers like this as an excuse not to go forward. That's probably why we don't have more speakers on the stages of the world! (Just kidding.)

The answer, however, is not what keeps people from speaking or from anything else for that matter. It's just their *perception* of success.   I've learned that many who express their desires and dreams, are not willing to put forth the effort to realize them. They go into the rationalization mode, by telling themselves *rational lies!* They begin finding fault with their dreams.   They use the excuse that successful people always become successful at the expense of others. They start believing dreamstealing excuses like: Money is the root of all evil; It's lonely at the top; I'll lose all my friends; and on and on and on....

The truth is, they aren't willing to do whatever it takes to make it happen. Plain and simple. If they would put as much effort into achieving as they have expended putting down the achievers and making excuses, they would be on their way to making their dreams come true. They would also be making a big difference in the lives of others.

What Is Success and What About Money?

Success is a journey, not a destination! Along the way we enjoy continuous triumphs, like helping a friend do something. We put in a day's work and forget about the effort and fatigue. We're thinking about what we have accomplished and what we're going to do next. It's not looking back at our regrets or down at others who haven't chosen to come with us, but looking ahead, staying focused on our dream and where we're going. It's realizing that money is not the root of *all* evil, but that *loving* money is only *one* of the *roots* of evil. Money is not evil in and of itself – it's just a tool – a medium of exchange. It can be used to do good or evil at the choice of the person who has it. This world will be a better place when more good people have more money.

Money buys food, builds churches and hospitals, and is the only thing that will do what it does. Having more than enough money removes the worry about paying the bills and gives us the freedom to really serve and be who we were created to be. Remember, the poor can't feed the poor.

If having money leads to some friends drifting away, which is highly unlikely, they weren't true friends in the first place. Besides, in the process of becoming successful, you'll make lots of new friends. As we go through life we associate with different people. For instance, how many of your first grade friends are you friends with today?   It really isn't lonely at the top – the view is better, and the company is awesome.

Can I Really Make My Dreams Come True?

You may have been told throughout your life that having dreams is a waste of time; forget them, and just focus on your job. Yet everything you come in contact with today started as somebody's dream. Did you ever consider that *you* are probably somebody's dream?

Your mind has incredible capabilities. It can develop ideas and dream dreams nobody else can. Yet it is also equipped with a governor. On an engine, a governor would limit the RPMs (revolutions per minute) so it can't turn fast enough to be damaged. Rental truck engines often have a governor. For example, no matter how much gas you give them, they will never go faster than the speed where they're set (which is often the speed limit).

Your may think I'm telling you you're limited. Yes you are, but only in a positive sense. Your mind will only come up with any ideas you can accomplish! That's why you didn't invent the light bulb, or find a cure for polio. Those were dreams given to others to pursue. You're equipped to do other things. While that may sound like a put-down, consider this: Every thought you ever had or have IS possible for you to turn into reality! For example, if you dream of a more exciting career, greater wealth, and better relationships, these are all possible. Anything is possible if you can think it. As Napoleon Hill said in his classic book *Think and Grow Rich,* "What the mind can conceive and believe it can achieve." *Your mind can only think of things that are possible for you to achieve, as long as you believe it!*

How Can I Make It Happen?

The secret to making it happen is to *focus.* Start with the thought and make it a dream. Demand that it happen; set goals, then *focus* on achieving them – no matter what. Forget about how "hard" it could be. Forget about what others will think, say, or do. Focus on the dream "why" and the "how" (to do it) will eventually make itself known to you.

Take your mind off of the *price* and concentrate only on the *prize;* and your success journey will begin. When you start on your path, you will be amazed at how many people will come to your aid to help you achieve it. *Misery may love company but success throws a better party!* Everyone is invited. Are you going, or do you have an excuse?

Focus on what you really, really, really want. That's what defines *your* success, and it's a very personal thing. Focus on it constantly so it stays in view. Keep in mind what you really want over a long period of time. This provides you with a clearer, more detailed picture of it.

Dreambuild

Go see your dream house, drive your favorite car, and watch a video of your favorite dream vacation. *Put pictures of what you want where you see them daily – on your refrigerator, in your car, on your bathroom mirror, by your bed, and in your office.* When your dream becomes crystal clear, you'll find the way to have it. Many valuable things, ideas, and people will come into your life along the line to help you. It's incredible, but you don't always have to "look" for them. Your enthusiasm *attracts* them! Consider them a bonus for keeping yourself committed to your dream. It's your driving force. As international business leader and author, Dexter Yager says, "Having a dream transports you out of the frustrations of the present into the possibilities of the future."

If you keep looking alongside the road, hoping to spot your prize, rather than focusing ahead, you'll be disappointed. The best thing that can possibly happen is that your trip will take a whole lot longer. More than likely though, you will end up in a ditch or totally lost. Most who reach this point lose hope, abandon the journey, turn around, and head for home. They can't wait to arrive and tell everyone within earshot that the trip was a waste of time and those who look to succeed are just fooling themselves. You can choose to never get your hopes up, so you won't be disappointed. As you may recall, that's called "a life of quiet desperation." If you keep doing what you're doing, while expecting a different result, that's akin to insanity; rather than saying, "We'll see what happens," you need to make it happen!

What Makes Other People Successful?

If you summed it up in one word, it would have to be "focus." If you were to interview the "other people," I would bet that, in many cases, they never even noticed you. It wasn't due to a lack of courtesy. It wasn't because they were successful and you weren't. It was because they were *focused* on their dream. It was irrelevant to them what your status was. They needed to pay attention to their goal and not worry about how they compared with you. Their eyes stayed pointed in the direction they were headed. They weren't off to the side looking for little pleasures or instant gratification so they could cope with their current circumstances. Successful people make their own circumstances. They "get-over-it" and "get-on-with-it."

Along the line, the focused people had their pockets filled up. They were filled with feelings of self-worth and self-esteem for accomplishing their goals in spite of the odds. They were overflowing with love and compassion because they had helped others along the way, rather than using them. They actually created "shortcuts" for the other travelers as they shared the principles of their success. They are kind, caring and other-centered. They want what's best for everyone concerned.

When their dreams came true, they didn't question the outcome by asking, "Is that all there is?" Instead they took satisfaction in the realization that success lies in the journey, not the destination. They also understand that future successes begin with but a single step in another direction, toward a different dream.

Don't Compare Yourself With Others

If all you do is compare yourself with others, you may "win" some, but you'll lose more. The best you can hope for is second place in *their* dream. As mentioned before, comparing is value judging which will injure your self-esteem, self-confidence, and ability to give and receive. Without those, you can't really succeed!

You need to *focus* on *your* dream. *Let go of any concern about what others may think.* They don't pay your bills! You won't be ignoring the important people in your life. As a matter of fact, they're likely to be right by your side helping you along the way. If they don't support you in the beginning, it may be that they don't understand what you're doing. As you show them you're committed and you start getting results, they're more likely to come around and support you.

Once you become focused and take appropriate action, your outcomes *will* change. You'll begin to attract the people you need to accomplish your dream. Opportunities to meet them will seem to spring up from nowhere. By focusing on *your dream,* you will actually help more people than you ever could by watching someone else live their dream. After all, life is not a spectator sport; it requires doing something.

If you want success, you need to become the "other person" for all the average people out there. The best way to solve the "average people problem" is to not be one of them! By your example, you will lead others out of mediocrity.

"The person who makes a success of living is the one who sees his goals and aims for it unswervingly. That is dedication."
Cecile B. DeMille

C

Chapter 12

CALLING FOR PRESSURE
The Twelfth Secret of the NO REJECTION Process

"It is not in the still calm of life, or in the repose of a pacific station, that great characters are formed... Great necessities call out great virtues."
Abigail Adams

How Do You Handle Pressure?

Have you ever had the desire to move to the country to escape the pressures of everyday life? I sure did. So a number of years ago my wife, Helen, and I packed up and did just that. We bought a house in the country and began raising a family. Unfortunately, pressure must have gotten tired of big city life as well. It seemed to follow us here! As each of our children were born and we needed to make improvements to the house, pressure came-a-calling. When we needed a new vehicle, pressure came with the payment book. It seemed like every time we wanted to improve our lot in life, pressure returned.

Life Without Pressure?

I found that the only way to avoid pressure is to stop developing and improving your situation. Stay satisfied with the status quo – "same old, same old." Be thankful for what you have, and let it go at that. Avoid upsetting the apple cart. Most of all, whatever you do, avoid rejection. If you're careful not to do anything different than anyone else, much of the pressure you have been facing will disappear. You could choose to live this way, but it's likely to be average and boring.

Did you ever watch a space science fiction movie? At least one person meets their doom when their spacesuit gets cut open while they are floating around some planet. What happens? Their body expands until they explode. Why? In space there's a vacuum; there's no pressure.

To some degree, the same thing can happen in real life. If you live life without any pressure, you will "explode" into nothingness. Pressure holds us together. Fortunately, much of it is self-imposed. How we regulate and deal with it helps determine the quality of our lives. *Remember, a chunk of coal is a diamond in a low pressure situation!*

How Does Being Prepared Affect Your Pressure?

Which would you rather have, the opportunity to invite someone to your home at a mutually suitable time, or have a sudden, unexpected knock at the door when you're in your pajamas? Obviously, if you took the time to invite someone, you would be ready for them. You would be able to comfortably see and deal with them on *your* terms. If it was a social visit, you would set the tone by determining what games and entertainment would be used. If it was a business meeting you called, you would have the advantage because you would have set and prepared the topic of discussion. It's also on your turf, where you're most comfortable. How well would you handle it if the shoe were on the other foot? What if you had less control and were vulnerable to someone else's agenda and environment?

If someone caught you totally unprepared, either socially or in business, would you entertain them with ease or put yourself under a lot of pressure? Chances are, if you allowed yourself to get rattled, these uninvited guests would be able to set the tempo of the entire visit. Being unprepared, you may decide you're not in a position to do much about it. The best you could hope for is to get through it as painlessly as possible. Would you have the self-esteem to take charge? Would you acknowledge that you're unprepared and tell them what you've got to offer and that's it?

The Effects of Pressure Depends On Your Attitude

Depending on your attitude, you may not feel any more pressure having spontaneous guests than if you were prepared for them. Being totally flexible helps. You may even enjoy it more without the pressure of preparation. The only real difference is who's in control. Are you the one controlling the pressure (inviting and preparing), or are you the one allowing yourself to be controlled by the pressure (surprise guests)? You could choose the attitude that you'll just relax, enjoy your guests, and not make a fuss. Since people are always coming in and out of our lives, it's better to invite them on our terms rather than having them just show up. Even so, an unexpected visit once in a while may be a welcomed change in your routine.

In one form or another, we often come in contact with pressure whether we impose it on ourselves or someone else attempts to impose it on us. When we are not prepared, we need to be careful not to let pressure get to us. We may have a knee-jerk (automatic) reaction,   feel defenseless, and consequently let pressure dictate the rules.   You may feel forced to stay in a dead-end job due to a surprise financial pressure. Yet, when you look at it as your choice (so you can stay financially afloat) and that it's only temporary, you're less likely to feel the pressure.

You may have overextended yourself due to your self-imposed pressure of "keeping-up-with-the-Jones's."   You may sell yourself short just to get a job when the pressures of a surprise layoff force you to move on.   Reduce your pressure by realizing your biggest benefit will rise out of your difficulties. As Napoleon Hill says in *Think and Grow Rich,* "In every adversity lies the seed of an equal or greater benefit."

Pressure can be a catalyst for us to do things; but it can also create problems.   Health can often be affected by surprise pressure.   Heart attacks are often attributed to tensions brought on by undo and unprepared for pressure. They can also be the result of the pressure of everyday life – if we allow it to control us.

Pressure can come from any direction, even as a response to inactivity. When my dad had a heart attack years ago, it wasn't because of the responsibilities he had as a business owner. At that time, doctors dealt with heart attack patients by insisting they have absolute quiet and none of the "pressures" of business.   Years later we learned that Dad's heart attack was caused by his diet and lifestyle.   Lying around waiting to heal was not my father's style. While the doctor insisted he avoid the day-to-day turmoil of running a business, he thrived on the pressures of deadlines, customer expectations, and suppliers. He actually took it all in stride. In fact, the inactivity of his recuperation almost killed him! He finally ignored the doctor and began handling big contracts again.   His recovery went a lot faster once he started working under pressure – the kind he liked.

Invite Pressure

When we invite pressure, we can use it to our advantage! It can serve us not only when it arrives under our terms and conditions but also when it doesn't!   *No matter how the pressure is created, it can be the catalyst for action.*   It's important to remember that. The difference in the outcomes from either invited or uninvited pressure is totally in the choices we make about how pressure will affect us.

To rise to the top quickly, you need to invite pressure. When you consciously choose to face the fear of rejection, you can deal with it on *your* terms.   Fear of rejection is a type of pressure.   We may allow it to be an excuse not to do something and stay "stuck."   But spending a lot of energy avoiding rejection, leaves us little or no energy to prepare for or deal with it.   Rejection often comes when you least expect it, on its own terms.   Maintaining intact self-esteem, being flexible, and knowing rejection is beneficial, helps you persist through and beyond the rejection experience.

Commit to Doing Your Best

Once you understand rejection is a learning tool and use it to further your success, you will be ready when it comes and you'll use it to grow.   For example, when I write a book, I *know* it will be published.   I believe that with all my heart.   I put all my effort into and commit to writing a quality piece. When I am finished, I visualize it in bookstores and people's homes everywhere.   The only thing I can't see is which publisher will produce my work.   If I feared rejection, I would try to guess the one publisher who would be perfect for me and send the manuscript only to them, and wait.

If I went to the mailbox expecting a contract and a check from that one publisher, and got nothing but a rejection letter, my dream might explode into a thousand pieces. I might not want to go through *that* again so I may decide never to send it to another publisher. I could "content" myself by wondering every now and then about what might have been. Besides, if I picked the one publisher I thought would be perfect for my book, I would have convinced myself there would be no one else out there who might consider it. By choosing to avoid the chance of being rejected again, I'd be "safe" but sorry.

I chose a different way. Since I am an author and not a publisher, I choose to do what I do best – write. Publishers consider many things before publishing a book. Timing, other books on the topic, marketing, and other factors enter the picture. What is inappropriate for one publisher is sometimes wonderful for another. Learning this, I decided to invite rejection and pressure. I sent the manuscript to as many publishers as possible so I could deal with them on *my terms*. I knew that most of them would probably reject my work, but I also knew that only one of them had to say "yes" for my dream to come true. From the moment I mailed the first copy of the manuscript, I knew I had total control over my *response* to rejection and pressure. I decided to relax with it, knowing it was just part of the game *I chose* to play.

How To Invite and Control Pressure

How do you invite and control pressure? The next time you set a goal that you really want to achieve, do yourself a big favor – tell someone. Pick someone special to you and tell them about your dream. A true friend, your spouse, or another confidant, would be great choices. Don't pick someone who agrees with you just because they think it's a nice thing to do. You need someone who will offer support and encouragement, who'll also keep checking to see how you are doing. The check-up part is inviting pressure. As Rich DeVos said in his book *Compassionate Capitalism*, "If you are serious about meeting your goals, telling the world in clear and certain terms will help you meet them. At least you should confide your goals to somebody who'll encourage and confront you along the way."

Certain people you pick could be negative. There are those who will try to put your goal down. Be prepared if it happens; it probably will. Consider it as just another rejection for you to grow through. Use this pressure to strengthen your resolve. Keep in mind that their rejection is about them. It could be that they don't think they could reach your goal, so therefore they don't believe you can either. Go prove them wrong.

Pressure From Supportive People Helps You Grow

True supporters won't let you get away with making excuses. They will help you get through temporary setbacks. They will believe in you and your ability to achieve your dream. They will pat you on the back when you deserve it, and always cheer you on. True supporters will be with you through "good" times and "bad." They will point out your mistakes and also give you honest compliments.

Such supportive people help you drive yourself on to completing your task. The suggestions they give you are sincere, and they would never say anything deliberately to discourage you. Any "rejection" of your ideas they offer are likely to be constructive and need to be considered heavily before you move-on. They'll ask you key questions to help you do what's best for you. You need *some* pressure and these people will help provide it. Proper pressure will help grow you into the person you were destined to be.

The Difference Between a Chunk of Coal and a Diamond

When I give smaller seminars to 50 or so people, here's an exercise I like to use. I hand out a rock to each participant and ask them to describe it. I'm lucky if 1 out of 50 gets the point. The other 98% will describe only what they see, a chunk of coal. The one that gets it right might say – it's a diamond in training, in the rough, in development, or in disguise.

Without pressure, the rock will always be a lump of coal. It can provide a minute's worth of heat; but after that it doesn't have much value. With the right amount of pressure, over an extended period of time, it will become a precious gem valued throughout the world. Are you like that lump of coal? Are you waiting just for that one moment to give up your "heat" for fear of losing your value? Or are you sending out invitations to pressure and rejection? When you continue to invite pressure and rejection, it is only a matter of time before the world will have one more precious gem to admire and share.

Change Is Inevitable, Growth Is Optional

We never need to seek pressure directly. It occurs every time we do something different to create a positive change. Change is a part of life and it always creates pressure. We all need change. We all need to change something in our lives to create the different results we want. Change will happen, to some degree anyway, because life is change. We might as well take charge of it, invite pressure and rejection, and move in the direction of our dreams. *Change is inevitable, growth is optional.*

"The most significant change in a person's life is a change of attitude – right attitudes provide right actions."
William J. Johnston

Chapter 13

ACT "AS IF" YOU'RE AN ACCEPTANCE MAGNET

The Thirteenth Secret of the NO REJECTION Process

"The world is a great mirror. It reflects back to you what you are. If you are loving, if you are friendly, if you are helpful, the world will prove loving and friendly and helpful to you. The world is what you are."
Thomas Drier

Think Acceptance!

You can minimize rejection by thinking acceptance. End of chapter. It's probably that simple, but let me give you your money's worth. Pay careful attention to this. You will not be able to avoid rejection simply by telling yourself NOT to think about it. It is impossible not to think about something just by making a conscious decision not to think about it! You need to replace it with something else; you need to fill the void. *Focus only on <u>what you want.</u>* Whatever's on your mind has the distinct possibility of happening. The following scenario is an excellent example.

It's the bottom of the ninth with two out. You are ahead by one run and the opposing team has runners on second and third. The catcher calls time and approaches the pitcher. On the mound they discuss the hitter. The catcher says, "He loves the pitch high and inside. Whatever you do don't throw one high and inside." He walks back to home plate, flashes the signal, the pitcher nods, winds up, and throws. Where do you suppose the pitch ended up? Out of the park. That's where. The pitcher focused on "high and inside." The catcher could have told the pitcher to pitch it low and outside to get the pitcher's mind focused on where it needs to be. Thoughts turn into reality. *It's important to think about what you want,* not what you don't want! Don't believe me? Try this....

On the count of three, and for the next thirty seconds, concentrate on one thing and one thing only. Put down this book as soon as you finish the instructions and look at the clock. Check the time. For the next thirty seconds you must absolutely *not* be thinking of a big blue elephant. GO!

That big blue elephant you are not thinking of – is it dark blue or light blue? To further prove my point, is it not there at the circus or not there in the jungle? Telling ourselves not to do or think about something makes it that much clearer in our minds! It's the same thing with rejection. Telling ourselves that it is not going to happen makes it that much clearer in our minds that we're concerned about it happening. That's what we project to others and therefore, that's what we attract!

Did someone ever try to sell you something and you knew within seconds that they didn't believe you would say "yes"? They were expecting rejection. It may not be as obvious as them saying, "I know you're probably not interested...." However, their focus was either on previous rejections or the misguidance of someone telling them not to even think of rejection. They may have been told to simply put rejection out of their mind. That only served to make it a clearer presence which became part of their outward mannerisms. They projected rejection. Since few people like to deal with rejection, it's no wonder that projecting rejection turns people off. The recipient then rejects the projector!

If you needed to sell cars to make a living, would you ever greet a customer by asking, "You wouldn't want to buy a car today would you"? Not many cars get sold that way. Anyone who asks that question will get rejected almost 100% of the time.

Project Acceptance, Unattachment, and a Win-Win Attitude

You always get back what you project. If you project a sense of impending rejection you'll almost certainly be rejected. If you believe most people will tell you "no," you tend to focus on the "noes." When you focus on the "yesses," you'll blast through the "noes" better and achieve success sooner. What attitude are you projecting? If you want failure, think and project rejection. *When you're ready for success, think and project acceptance.*

Maintain a positive attitude that you'll be liked and accepted. Stay focused on the needs of your customers and creating a win-win situation. You're unattached to making the sale. It's OK either way with you. You'll create a comfortable climate for your customers to decide what's best for them. As Frank Bettger says in his book *How I Raised Myself From Failure to Success in Selling,* "See things from the other person's point of view and talk in terms of his (or her) wants, needs, desires."

Be other-centered and focus on your customer. Everybody is broadcasting on radio station WII-FM (What's In It-For Me?) so you need to tune-in to that station. As Zig Ziglar

says, "People don't care how much you know until they
know how much you care..." Many times salespeople are
taught never to take "no" for an answer. This is a big
mistake! Whenever the customer says they don't want to
buy, many salespeople take a *position*; they usually defend
their product or service. (In this situation, or even just in a
conversation when each party takes a different position, the
natural tendency is to defend it to the end.) The result is
usually that nothing gets sold that day, and the salesperson
never satisfies the customer's needs. It happened all because
the salesperson was taught never to take "no" for an answer.

Gather Those "Noes" and Find Out Why

When you seek success, you need to get as many "noes" as
you can. Once you have them, handling them properly is
key. If you were to find out why someone said "no" to you,
would you be better or worse off? The answer is better.
You'd then have an objection you may be able to satisfy,
even if it's with another option. Or, you may learn how to
fine-tune your approach for future reference.

Don't get into a battle of wills; it can't be won. As Dale
Carnegie once said, "A man convinced against his will is of
the same opinion still." Instead, earn the privilege of being
able to further probe for an answer that benefits both you and
your customer.   You'll benefit because what you are
presenting (an opportunity, goods, services, or even your
opinion) has a better chance of being happily received. The
benefit to your customer is they are satisfied that all their
needs have been met (by you directly or by your referral to
someone else) and their questions have been answered. The
greatest benefit is *both* sides won. Even if an actual sale isn't
made, the relationship is intact. As Abraham Lincoln once
said, "Am I not destroying my enemies when I make friends
of them?"

Dilute It

How do you project acceptance and get rejection out of your mind, without concentrating on the rejection? A friend of mine gave me a great analogy. Let's say rejection came in the form of vinegar and I told you that, in order to be successful, you needed to drink a cup of it. Could you do it? Vinegar, like rejection, is hard to swallow; it's very bitter. However what if we took that cup of vinegar and poured it into a 55 gallon drum of cold spring water; could you then drink it? Of course you could! Once it was diluted by 55 gallons of water, you wouldn't taste any bitterness.

Treat rejection that way. You'll never be totally free of any thoughts of rejection, unless you've never experienced any. If you don't recall ever being rejected, it probably means you are either denying it or aren't part of the human race!

When you have the attitude that you'll do whatever it takes to be successful and each attempt is a learning experience, you've already changed your focus to one of acceptance. By giving your mind something else to focus on, you'll begin diluting any rejection you may have experienced in the past. You're diluting rejection thoughts by adding acceptance thoughts. This will cause you to focus more easily on the outcome you desire. What could be simpler?

Reverse the Process – *Take It Away!*

Another person I know who is quite successful, has a unique way of approaching rejection. He puts the "pressure" on the person doing the rejecting! He is involved in sales and is one of the top producers in his field. Let's call him Alan. As a sales trainer, I always seek out top performers so that I might learn from them. I asked Alan what he attributed his great success to, and he was kind enough to share it with me.

Whenever he sells a product, he is low key and simply explains all the benefits to the buyer. His posture is that everyone needs what he has to offer. He believes he would be doing them a great disservice if he didn't show them how his products would benefit them.

Alan never creates a high pressure situation with any potential customer. I asked him, "When does he stop selling?" His reply was incredible. He simply explains all the reasons a customer needs to have his product.   In response to his posturizing attitude, they prove to him they need it! When they attempt to sell him on why they need what he has, HE REJECTS THEM – by taking it away from them! He pushes them back. The key is that *people want what they don't think they can have.* It's just human nature. That's having the right focus!

Here's a quote from Napoleon Hill – *"When men first come in contact with crime, they abhor it. If they remain in contact with crime for a time, they become accustomed to it, and endure it. If they remain in contact with it long enough, they finally embrace it."* Let's change the wording so that it fits our agenda. *"When children first come in contact with rejection, they abhor it. As they grow into adulthood, they become accustomed to it and endure it. If they remain in contact with it long enough, they soon embrace it and become totally influenced by it. After learning how to deal with it, they welcome it and grow from it."*

How Much Do You Choose Rejection?

Much of the rejection we attract to ourselves is, believe it or not, by choice! While few of us *consciously* choose rejection, it is our choice nonetheless. We need to dilute the thoughts of rejection in our mind by pouring positive ideas, lessons, desires, dreams, and goals into it. We then become "magnetized" to attract acceptance.   Like attracts like. Always keep your well of optimistic ideas and dreams full. Take all you need from it, using it as a resource to dilute the rejection.

As   long as you have the attitude that rejection is beneficial, you will never let it control you.   The only way any of us can fail is to quit.   Quitting is the ultimate rejection. If we quit, we reject ourselves!

In her book, *Feel the Fear and Do It Anyway,* Dr. Susan Jeffers explains that one of the foundations of fear is the belief that you can't handle whatever it is that you fear. The fact is that you *can* handle rejection. You don't need to let your fear stop you. You can *get beyond your fear.*   Take action, be unattached, focus on the needs of others, and have a positive, expectant attitude that you'll be liked and accepted.   Do this and you'll become an "Acceptance Magnet."

*"Events circumstances, etc. have their origin in ourselves.
They spring from the seeds which we have sown. "*
Henry David Thoreau

*"The greatest discovery of my generation is that man can
alter his life simply by altering his attitude of mind. "*
William James

Change your thoughts and you change your world. "
Norman Vincent Peale

Chapter 14

NOTHING CAN STOP YOU NOW!

The Fourteenth Secret of the NO REJECTION Process

"Nothing in the world can take the place of persistence. Talent will not; nothing is more common than unsuccessful men with talent. Genius will not; unrewarded genius is almost a proverb. Education alone will not; the world is full of educated derelicts. Persistence and determination are omnipotent."

Calvin Coolidge

You're Getting Stronger and Stronger

Now that we have spent some time together, I believe you'll be receptive to something very important. From this point on, *every time you face rejection and deal with it, you get stronger.* Every time someone tells you it can't be done, you'll rush ahead, yelling for them to get out of the way, while you do it!

As the average people try to drag you down by asking you, "If it's so easy, why isn't everyone doing it?" you smile as you get it done and shrug, "I don't know." You can now look forward to visiting all the negative thinking people who laughed at you and said to come back when you're a success.

Every time you face rejection and deal with it, you're less afraid of it the next time. As you continue on your road to success, your lessened fear turns into anticipation. You realize that *each "no" brings you closer to your dream!* The more "noes" you get, the more you can fine-tune your skills and attitude, and the more successful you'll be. You willingly accept rejection because behind it is the success you may not have recognized before. You've continued to have faith in your own ability. You've developed your skills and you are about to be rewarded accordingly. I admire your triumph and I'm grateful I may have helped, even in the smallest way.

Focus On What You Want – Not Rejection

Life is not about getting there first. It is about arriving at *your* chosen destination in *your* time. Once you determine where you would like to be and start your trip, you'll discover the joys of life are found along the line. Once you have made a decision to succeed and are taking appropriate action, you are a successful person. You are traveling with a clear plan or map that will take you where you want to go. Each rejection along the way will serve to keep you on-track, help you make adjustments, and speed your travel.

Avoiding rejection not only slows you down, it also causes you to detour from your planned route. If you avoid rejection you'll simply wander through life like a ship without a rudder. *People who plan to succeed expect rejection along the way.* They may even be afraid of rejection. However, they are so focused on achieving their goals, they don't let that fear stand in their way. This is the importance of focus. This is why you need to find the overall purpose for your life. How can you best use your talents and follow your dreams? What goals can you set? What's in your heart? Focus with passion on whatever it is that makes your heart sing. Overcoming the fear of rejection will be a small price to pay for living the life you want.

"For anything worth having one must pay the price; the price is always work, patience, love, self-sacrifice."
John Burroughs

Part Three

YOUR

INVINCIBLE

ROOF

S

Chapter 15

SOME WILL, SOME WON'T, SO WHAT! WHO CARES?

The Fifteenth Secret of the NO REJECTION Process

"When the dream's big enough, the facts don't count."
Dexter Yager

Would Guarantees Make Everyone Successful?

What if I could guarantee you would face a thousand "noes" before you heard the "yesses" that would make you wealthy? How many "noes" would you listen to before you would quit? Of the many who would *say* a thousand, how many of you would quit well before the end?

Even if their success is assured, there are those who will never put forth the necessary effort. They'll often say, "Money isn't everything." While that's true, if you're looking for an excuse, you can substitute any desire for the word money. Even when it's *your* dream that is on the line, and I can prove you will have it by going through the "noes," a lot of you would still quit! People who use such excuses cheat themselves out of getting what they really want.

For those of you who are parents, if I said a thousand "noes" would lead to the "yes" that would provide for your children, how many of you would still quit? How many of you would try for a while, then justify your quitting by telling the world, "Kids need to fend for themselves"? Yet, when you continue and win, you will not only provide for your children but you will set an excellent example for them as well. However, even with a guarantee, many of you would still quit. Why?

Did you know that Colonel Sanders presented his now famous Kentucky Fried Chicken recipe to 1,009 restaurants before he got his *first* "yes"? Just think of it. Here was a 66 year old man with an old Chevy who was on Social Security. He began a whole new career and enterprise when most people are ready to "pack-it-in." Because he followed his dream, the world was given a tasty meal. Thousands of people also found employment, and many got wealthy.

Everyone has been told, there are no guarantees in life. I am here to tell you, as emphatically as I can, life is full of them. The one that always hits me the hardest is that if we give up, we can guarantee the results. How many "noes" do you need to get through before you get the big "yes"? I don't know. Whatever the numbers are, they will certainly prepare you for when the "yes" comes along.

I guarantee the number of "noes" you get before you find the big "yes" is irrelevant. It just doesn't matter. You keep on going, regardless.   I can also guarantee that anyone who makes excuses and gives up on their dream, will never reach their desired destination. Winning in life is like playing tennis. Nobody counts the number of times they have to hit the ball over the net to win. They just keep hitting.

There are no exacts, no special number of rejections that will always lead to success. There are averages, estimates, and even wild guesses, but no one can tell you how many rejections *you* need to face to reach your goals in life. Each rejection we do face, however, is a one-shot deal. Once you face that one, it cannot bother you again unless you let it. If there's a lesson to be learned from the rejection, and you haven't learned it, beware.   You can practically be guaranteed to repeat your mistake and experience another similar rejection. Face it, deal with it, learn from it, and move-on.

Rejections Are Steps To Success – Possibilities

Consider the beginning of a journey. As stated earlier, "Even the journey of a thousand miles begins with a single step." Each rejection is a step. How you deal with it will determine whether you are stepping closer to or further away from your objective.

The following line diagram demonstrates the possibility of rejection. It offers tremendous potential. If you recognize and make use of it for what it truly is, I can guarantee you success.

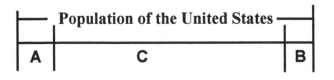

This line represents all the people in the country. Imagine, 261 million potential friends, benefactors, sales, clients, distributors, or customers, depending on what it is you are looking for. "A" represents 1% of the population. These people think, act, and want the same things you do. They're going to say "yes" to you just because you are the one who asked. That means your true potential is for 2.6 million friends, benefactors, sales, clients, distributors, or customers. Even at a dollar each, you would be wealthy. The only problem with this plan is, to guarantee full potential, you may have to talk to every man, woman, and child in America! That's not a very appealing thought.

"B" represents all of those who will never agree with anything you do. They are your opposites. I know the expression "opposites attract" is popular, but, I for one, never quite bought it. It works with magnets but seldom works on a long-term basis with people. For one thing, I don't find people or things very appealing that are opposite to my preferences.

Look at the world around you. Consider history. Do you think the Civil War was started because there was so much in common between the North and the South? They were exact opposites, not only geographically, but in their thinking.

There are people who will disagree with you simply because you're you and there's something they don't like about you. That's a fact! They represent about 10% of the population. You may think one solution is to avoid them. I don't think that's possible since many of them are often undercover and they seem to move around. Think for a moment. How would you recognize an opposite if you saw one? In most cases, you wouldn't!

The only thing positive for you about the opposites is now you can deal with their rejection. The next time you are rejected, and have made every reasonable effort to turn it around and learn from it, do this: Tell yourself that the person who rejected your idea was simply one of those who would have said "no" to anything you proposed. Two things will happen. First, you will not blame yourself, your product, or your idea for the rejection. Second, you won't spend additional time trying to convince them to change their mind.

Section "C" is everyone else; 89% of the population. These people have no preconceived opinion about you, your product, or your idea. They'll consider it on its own merit and be open to the possibility it could benefit them. They will evaluate it in their own way, get a feeling about it, and reach a decision. Their decision may be based totally on whether your product or idea can help them fill a particular need. They are not accepting or rejecting it based just on their opinion of you. These people may eventually grow to like you, your product, or your idea. They may like you a little and love your idea. They may despise you but be captivated by your idea. They may love you and hate your idea. They may hate you and hate your idea. Get the picture? Any outcome is possible with this group.

You need to meet, get to know, and present your proposal to them. They will evaluate it as best they can and make a decision they believe is right for them. I didn't say they would necessarily make the "right" decision, in *your* estimation. It is what *they believe* is right for them at that time. They could change their minds at any point in the future.

If you are rejected, give people the opportunity to change their minds without fear of embarrassment. Focus on *them*. Acknowledge that they need to do whatever they decide is best for them and that's fine with you. Your being other-centered will help them know you have their best interest at heart. You are unattached to the outcome and they can be relieved you aren't rejecting them for rejecting you! If you try to manipulate them into feeling guilty for saying "no" or show them negative emotion, you'll make it very difficult for them to come back to you.

There are over 231 million people in this last group. The truth is, they could decide either way – "yes" or "no." Your greatest potential for success lies here.   While positive answers may come easier   from your "A" group, once someone in your "C" group makes a decision, they generally stick with it. They become loyal because you respected them enough to give them all the facts and let them decide. Even the "C's" who say "no" are better for you. However, when a person from group "B" says "no," they will probably look to create more "noes" for you by spreading the word from their perspective. In group "C" they are probably saying, "No, not now." They could be a possibility for you later.

Which group do you want to focus on? Finding all of the "A's"? Avoiding all the "B's"? Concentrating on the big group of "C's"? No! You may consider it unfortunate, but these people don't wear uniforms. They don't meet you in alphabetical order either. You need to condition yourself to *talk to everyone until you reach your objective.* Opportunity will occur when you least expect it. When you understand who's potentially in the People Line, you are better prepared to stay on top of your game.

Act Like a Dog!

Dogs are great teachers. We have a black Lab named Vader at home, and I always enjoy watching him when new people visit. Each time a group sits in our living room, Vader begins making his rounds. Each new person gets the same amount of sniffing. Some people push him away because they don't like dogs. Others ignore him because they are paying attention to what someone else is saying or doing. Finally, a new visitor begins petting Vader on the head. Once that's going well, Vader flops down on his back. He loves to have his belly scratched. The person who began petting him is soon on the floor, rubbing Vader's belly. Both are happy with the decision.

Now why do you suppose Vader didn't just go to the middle of the room and lie down on his back and wait? He knew he stood a better chance of success if he allowed everyone the opportunity to participate. Besides, there is always the possibility that more than one person would like to play. What if everyone wants to play? Consider the possibilities!

Find Those "Yesses"

If you honestly think about everything we have covered so far in this chapter, you can believe that all the "yesses" you could ever want are out there. You can also believe that the better the "yes" will be for you, the harder it may be to find. But you'll find it as long as you keep looking, asking, and fine-tuning your approach. I can guarantee it! If you are still having trouble with the concept of guaranteed success based on the law of averages, consider this: If you are looking for nothing, I can guarantee your results here as well.

Focus On Where You're Going

When you focus on your objective, you will rarely, if ever, think about those who told you "no." It's a great idea, however, to keep a record of their names and contact information in a notebook. This could be a valuable resource for you in case you do something that might change their minds, like succeed – for instance. If you can remember all those who have rejected you, you haven't been rejected enough. You may also be making a big deal out of the "noes." If you continue doing that, it's going to prevent you from moving-on.

The beauty of all this is that you are learning to recognize your true potential when you deal effectively with rejection and keep going. Once you understand that, you'll never allow rejection to hurt you or keep you from your dream. In fact, it can be one of your best friends.

SW, SW, SW! Who Cares?

When you're brave enough to have dreams, you're strong enough to overcome rejection. Each rejection will always bring you closer to your dream. You just need to handle it properly and learn any lesson it brings with it. Understand that rejection is just part of the journey and it helps keep you on-track. As you share your product, idea, or dream with others, **some will** accept it, while **some won't**. Of those who don't accept it, say, "**So what! Who cares?**" Learn what you can from it and move-on.

So, the next time you're faced with a new challenge in presenting your product or idea to others, look in the mirror and repeat this to yourself, out loud:

**SOME WILL,
SOME WON'T,
SO WHAT!
WHO CARES?**

When you start believing that, you will feel the power shift. Many people feel overpowered by the fear of rejection and they let it hold them back from where they want to go. By adopting the "SW, SW, SW!" philosophy, you'll move the power back where it belongs – to you! You have the power to choose. You decide who has the power to affect you. When you choose not to let rejection stop you, it can't; you're in the driver's seat. When you focus on finding those who **WILL**, you'll no longer let rejection slow you down. In fact, you will go faster once you realize each rejection brings you closer to your dreams. You become stronger and more resolved each time you handle rejection. Keep "going-through-the-numbers" to find the "yesses" that lead to your success.

"If you learn from defeat, you haven't really lost."
Author Unknown

"You measure the size of the accomplishment by the obstacles you had to overcome to reach your goals."
Booker T. Washington

"Anything worth doing is worth doing poorly until you can learn to do it well."
Steve Brown

Chapter 16

THE REAL DREAMSTEALER
SELF-REJECTION

The Sixteenth Secret of the NO REJECTION Process

"If you want to be respected by others the great thing is to respect yourself. Only by that, only by self-respect will you compel others to respect you."

Fyodor Dostoevsky

Did You Ever Reject Yourself?

Has anyone ever said anything to you like, "You know, you should try _____ ; I think you'd be very good at it"? For many of you the answer is probably "yes." The important question is, if it seems like their suggestion could help you, are you doing it or did you at least try? Most people respond with statements like, "Oh, I could never do that." Or, "Who me? No, I am not that type of person."

False modesty? Perhaps. In reality, though, it's probably self-rejection.

When you'd love the results of doing something and others believe you can do it, yet you still refuse, – that's self-rejection.   You may no longer believe in creating or accepting new ideas. Mentally, you may have been listing all the things you think you can't do, instead of all the things you can do. You may be putting yourself on the downward spiral of self-rejection. Everything happens for a reason – to benefit you – yet you may be failing to recognize it. You may be becoming a self-fulfilling prophesy of negative results. As each challenge occurs you may be giving in by saying to yourself, "I just knew that was gonna happen."

How can anyone honestly hope to succeed with an attitude like that?   Imagine how would you think and feel as a pilot boarding your airplane with that type of an attitude? As you pulled up to taxi onto the runway you would look at it and say, "I don't think I can do it." Upon checking your fuel, you'd feel sure the tank was empty, even though you filled it yourself. As you thought about advancing the throttle, you'd become convinced you'd make the engine fail. Even if you did get any momentum, you'd believe you couldn't make the airplane take off. And once you were flying, you'd be afraid your navigation equipment would probably fail (even though you inspected it) so you couldn't reach your destination.

You might think I'm stretching it here to make a point. Am I? Substitute *your* occupation for pilot and *your* normal routine for each of the steps in this story. If it's starting to sound familiar, you may be creating a pattern of self-rejection. The good news is, when we recognize this pattern, we can fix it. Self-rejection, like any other type of rejection, can be handled. Of course it's important to get and keep the attention of the person causing the rejection; you need to get *you* to pay attention. The cure is simple. It took you a long time to become accustomed to self-rejection, and it may take a while to overcome it. No matter how long it takes, it'll be worth it.

You don't simply replace what's already inside of you with something else. Your brain has stored everything you have ever heard, said, felt, seen, or done. Whether it is positive or negative, it's in there. What you *can* do is *dilute* it. As mentioned earlier, you can continue adding something else until there is barely a trace of the original. Even if you can add your new positive input in only small amounts at a time, it's still diluting the negative. Changing is a process and even small changes represent progress. It won't take much for you to notice a difference.

Do This

Stand up straight and put your shoulders back. Begin taking deep breaths. Keep your head up. Now put the biggest smile possible on your face. Without changing a thing about the way you look or breathe, act rejected. You can't, can you? When you do this for two minutes a day you'll begin feeling a positive difference. Is that all there is to it? Well, the next time you feel rejection coming on, do the above exercise, then you tell me. It's a great start to gaining more self-acceptance.

Take the Trip Back From Self-Rejection

People dealing with self-rejection often feel they don't have time to relax; they may do things at breakneck speed. Starting tomorrow, get up 15 minutes earlier, and do everything as you normally do. If everything occurs as it typically does, you'll have 15 extra minutes to relax before you leave home. What would you enjoy? Would it be breakfast with the kids? When was the last time you did that? Would you like to read from a positive book? Maybe it means you can have an extra cup of coffee or you can leisurely drink, rather than gulp the first cup. Or, you can even take a brisk walk. You *can* really do something for *you*. YOU CAN RELAX! Think how good having 15 undedicated minutes would feel. Go for it and start enjoying the experience tomorrow morning.

Self-rejected people are so busy, so certain that only negative things are going to happen, they become robotic. To avoid this, it helps to focus on the positive and be appreciative. Tonight, when you get ready for bed, make a list of reasons for getting-up tomorrow. Read them out loud. If you feel negative about any of them, cross them out and replace them with positive reasons. Keep refining your list until only the reasons you truly want are on it. Decide to be grateful; you have all those reasons to get up. An "attitude of gratitude," as Robert H. Schuller calls it, works miracles.

Birds of a Feather Flock Together

Most of us know what that means. We tend to hang around people like ourselves. When you decide to change, you need to change the crowd you associate with. Instead of growling, "What's that guy (or gal) so happy about?" – go over and find out. They may make a great new acquaintance or friend. Hanging around positive thinking people reduces the rejection you encounter. They'll encourage you to become rejection proof. You'll also have opportunities to express your ideas and get honest responses and constructive suggestions. You'll have people supporting and encouraging you to make your ideas work rather than people who just dump on your ideas and say they won't work.

You Are What You Eat

We tend to be more negative and self-rejecting when we feel sluggish. If you are working and eat a huge bulky lunch, by 2 PM you're likely to lose much of your desire to be productive. By 3 PM you'll probably be a "clock watcher" and that spells a self-rejection relapse. Eating a lunch high in carbohydrates gives you added energy in the afternoon. A good salad and pasta is not only filling, but it doesn't take long to digest and therefore doesn't tire you out. Find out what works best for you. Digestion can take more energy from your body than other activities, so the general recommendation is to eat light.

Imagine Being the Person You'd Like to Be

Tell yourself, "I'm a good person." Say it and mean it! Then list all the things that prove your point. Take your time on this one. The more detail the better. If you are drawing a blank or having a hard time getting started, imagine being the person you would like to be. Now list all of those qualities. Place a star next to the qualities you feel would be easy to have today. Adopt them and start acting that way immediately.

Accomplish Something

Set your sights on accomplishment. Once you have completed something, stand back and admire it. Let yourself know that no one else could have accomplished it quite the way you did. Do that with everything you finish, including all we have discussed so far. Admiring your accomplishments will help you go on to do more. But don't rest on your laurels. Fill your mind with a new goal. At that point there won't be any room for your or anyone else's rejection. You're now becoming "diluted" with the positive.

Here's a quote I often use to describe the value of hard work: *"It's what you do in the valleys that determines how long you can enjoy the view from the peaks."* Turbocharge

your dreams; focus like your life depends on it. Go for it.
THINK PEAKS!

Get Injected With Goals

Self-rejection can become a serious disease. And like
many diseases, there is a vaccination that will lessen the
effects or even prevent it from occurring. In this case the
vaccine is goal setting. *Goals can help protect us from self-
rejection.* We need something to "shoot" for. If we don't
have goals, the world will put us in slots designed for others
rather than letting us find our own spot. For self-rejection to
take hold and spread throughout your thinking, it needs to
have your focus. When you are focused on your goal, such
rejection will have a hard time getting your attention. Even
if self-rejection can get you to notice it, a goal can prevent it
from getting a stronghold on you. Then the rejection will
just whither and die.

Goals help you stay on course so you can achieve your
dreams. They give you something to work toward every day.
Goals need to be something you go toward, not something
you are escaping. Set goals, want them with a passion, and
focus on getting them. Get whatever help you need and do
what it takes to achieve them. When you commit to and do
all of this, it will be impossible for you to become a victim of
self-rejection.

Don't let anybody, especially yourself, steal your dream!

*"Winners evaluate themselves in a positive manner and look
for their strengths as they work to overcome weaknesses."*
Zig Ziglar

*"Having a long term goal provides a catalyst for motivation
at every waking moment."*
Peter Daniels

Chapter 17

ON THE RIGHT TRACK
The Seventeenth Secret of the NO REJECTION Process

"When you win, nothing hurts."

Joe Namath

Are You Still In the Game?

You have read about different types of rejection and may be saying to yourself, "I could be an expert with all the rejection I've gone through." You may be right. However, answering the next question is far more important in determining your future than understanding all the rejection you have gone through. *What are you doing today?*

When you're giving your best to win, be sure to consult with those that are where you want to be. Do that, stay in the game, and go for your dream, and you'll be well on your way to becoming an expert at handling rejection. For you this message provides a few pointers, but more importantly, it confirms that you need to keep going. You *are* on the right track.

If you think you're defeated, you'll lose. If you've had difficulty staying focused, or you've been duped into believing dreamers never win, you may become an armchair quarterback. You may be calling the plays based on hindsight and the uneducated opinions of others.

The good news is that since you've read this far, you realize change is the only way to grow. You've decided you're willing to change and you're going to do it. Right? As professional speaker and TV host, Ty Boyd says, "...So it is more than willingness to change that sets the true leaders apart. It is seeking out change and wringing every bit of potential out of it that takes you to the next horizon in your growth."

You're beginning to realize it's possible for *you* to win. Of course you can win only when you play the game. When you decide you are ready, do it with the intensity of a champion. Some of you may think that sounds like a lot of positive thinking junk. But when an underdog upsets the favorite, what do you suppose they thought about during the entire game? Was it the previous loss? Was it the greatness of the opponent? No! All they ever thought about was *winning*. None of the coaches I know of have ever asked their teams to "keep it close" since they were going to lose anyway!

Are You In a Rut?

Are you willing to play to win every day? Some people say "No." They're willing to "settle for" the way things are. They've chosen to give up on making things better. Each day they go to work and do an average job for an average wage.   They come home, complain about the world in general, and fall asleep in front of the TV. The next day they wake up, go to work, do an average job for an average wage, come home, complain about the world in general, fall asleep in front of the TV. The next day they wake up and go to work and on and on and on.... Yuck! Sure sounds like a rut, doesn't it?

Picture a strip of land as your path to your daily routine or job. Consider what would happen to that strip if you kept pacing back and forth for 40 years. How far down would you compress it? Maybe six feet? Can you picture it? Now picture hundreds of these scenes side by side, row after row. When you're breathing, they call it a rut. If not, they call it a grave. A rut is just a grave with the ends kicked out!

As I've said before, cemeteries are the sources of more unrecoverable natural resources than any other places in the world. They hold buried dreams, inventions, symphonies, cures, and just plain joy that will never be shared. I have heard it said that most people lose their dreams and mentally "die" by age 25, but their bodies keep going for another 40 to 75 years! It's worth repeating what the *Bible* says, "Where there is no vision, the people perish."

What Will You Leave Behind To Grow?

I once heard a definition of Hell I'll always remember. Picture yourself, when your time comes, meeting St. Peter at the Pearly Gates and he says, "Before I take you to meet God, I have someone special for you to meet." Slowly, from out of the mist, a figure appears. This person is obviously happy, and is surrounded by a large crowd of admirers.

As the figure gets closer, you start to feel uneasy. That person looks just like you! St. Peter says, "I'd like you to meet the person you could have become." You get a deep chill.

To me, that would be the ultimate punishment – to see what you could have become and how many people you could have helped had you learned to deal with rejection and gone for your dreams.   To know you could have been rewarded with your dream home, more time with your family, those special trips you could have taken, and whatever other rewards you could have been blessed with had you only served more.   What an incredible disappointment to finally realize you could have made a difference in the world, but *chose* not to. What a shame.

But that's not going to happen to you! You're going to "grab-the-bull-by-the-horns" and do whatever it takes to overcome your fears of rejection and make your dreams come true.   This poem by Edgar Guest brings home a message we all need to remember....

TOMORROW

He was born to be all a mortal could be–
Tomorrow
None should be stronger or braver than he–
Tomorrow
A friend who was troubled and weary, he knew,
Who'd be glad of a lift – and needed it too
On him he would call to see what he could do –
Tomorrow
Each morning he'd stack up the letters he'd write–
Tomorrow
And he thought of the friends he'd fill with delight–
Tomorrow
It was too bad indeed he was busy today
And hadn't a moment to stop on his way
More time I'll give to the others he'd say –
Tomorrow
The greatest of workers this man would have been –
Tomorrow
And the world would have known him had he ever seen –

Tomorrow
But the fact is, he died and faded from view
And all that was left here when living was through
Was a mountain of things he intended to do –
Tomorrow

What's Behind Procrastination?

I have shared that poem with many people and they all initially agree that it's about procrastination. They are right, to a point. But we need to go deeper. Why procrastinate? Some people say they put off something to avoid the chance someone will be angry with them. That's avoiding rejection. Others believe that if they wait, the circumstances will change, and the opportunity will get better. That could be just an excuse to reject the idea. The rest feel that if they wait long enough, the situation will fade away and they won't have to deal with it. They have effectively avoided rejection, at least for the moment. No matter how you slice it, the problem is often a fear of rejection – fear of other people and what they will think, say, or do.

Do You Want To Accelerate Your "Yesses"?

The good news is that, by coming this far in the process, you are already on the path of overcoming those fears. To encourage you even further, I don't know of anyone who has ever died from rejection. The word "no" doesn't come with a warning label saying – "It's hazardous to your health"! It simply gives you choices. You can either stay and do your best to change the "noes" to "yesses," or you can simply go on to the next person and ask the same question. It depends on the situation. As you increase your effectiveness and continue to talk to people about your idea, sooner or later you'll begin getting the "yesses" you deserve. Whether it's sooner or later, depends largely on you.

For example, let's say a particular car salesperson is having a tough time selling enough cars to make a living. They're ready to quit. You find out that for every 10 people they talk to, they are able to sell a car. They need to sell 20 cars a month to make the kind of money they desire. Simple math tells you they need to talk to 200 people each month to earn what they want. When they are determined to win, nothing will prevent them from talking to 200 people. Yet most people are in a "rut" – they keep doing the same things, getting the same undesirable results. How come? Coming from the car business I can tell you some of the losing excuses I've heard as well as winning reasons.

Losing excuse – "We don't get that many customers through the door."

Winning reason – "I'm making a bunch of phone calls."

Losing excuse – "They want ME to make appointments? They should advertise more."

Winning reason – "I make lots of phone calls. The people who show up from ads are a bonus."

Losing excuse – "The boss is trying to sell these cars for more than the competition."

Winning reason – "I hope they keep selling at this price; I'm earning more money."

Both the folks offering winning reasons as well as those giving losing excuses could be extremely nice people. However, those making excuses are setting themselves up for rejection. The others are setting themselves up for acceptance. The excuse- makers focus only on the task as labor. The winners focus on the *desired outcome*. They consider the task only as one of the ingredients. One group makes excuses, while the other MAKES THINGS HAPPEN and has more control over the results.

When you believe you're in either group, you're training to win. Even if you currently fear rejection and you're making excuses, the fact that you can recognize this gives you hope. In fact, if you realize you're afraid of rejection, congratulations, you are 75% cured. You just need to take the proper dose of "medicine" and you will be winning in no time.

"Plan your work for today, then work your plan."
Norman Vincent Peale

"Man must cease attributing his problems to his environment, and learn again to exercise his will – his personal responsibility."
Albert Schweitzer

P

Chapter 18

PERCEPTION IS "REALITY"

The Eighteenth Secret of the NO REJECTION Process

"I would rather attempt something great and fail, than to attempt to do nothing and succeed."
Robert H. Schuller

Whatever You Believe Is Your Reality

By now, some of you may be wondering if any of these ideas work in the real world. Do ordinary humans, mere mortals, believe this stuff? The important question is, "Do *you* believe it?" With anything you don't physically see, i.e., the intangible, it's the presenter's belief that's the most convincing. Your *confidence* in what you're saying is, in many cases, more powerful than the message.

How To Promote Acceptance

Now let's consider a real life situation, complete with real rejection, that comes to a mutually beneficial end. I'll use an actual example from seminars I've given over the years.

You are presenting an opportunity to someone. It would allow them to build a new business part-time while they maintained their present job or business. Once the new business grows and prospers to a certain level, they can retire from what they're currently doing, if they choose to. The presenter we'll call "businessperson" and the person being presented to we'll call "prospect." We'll pick-up after the presentation, evaluate it, and discover whether there is acceptance or rejection.

Businessperson – "I would like your opinion on whether or not you think there's any benefit for you to take advantage of the opportunity I've just shared with you."

Prospect – "No."

Businessperson – "I'm sure you have a reason for feeling that way. May I ask what it is?"

Prospect – "I'm too busy. I don't have time for this."

Businessperson – "I understand. Imagine, if you will, having all the time in the world, then could you see the potential in this concept?"

Prospect – "Yes, I suppose there is potential. But as I've said, I don't have enough time."

Businessperson – "I understand. In fact I have met others who also said lack of time was an obstacle. But I guess that brings up a question - Is there really enough potential in my plan in spite of your concerns about time? Is that the question?"

Prospect – "Yes."

We could continue, but at this point we're going to review exactly what was said and why the businessperson answered the way they did.

The first thing the businessperson wanted from the prospect, after they showed them their opportunity, was an opinion. When asked, most people will give an opinion on just about anything. In many sales training sessions, I was taught to never ask questions that could be answered with a "yes" or a "no." I have since learned that people have become much more sophisticated. They may resent this approach, which could lead to rejection.

Avoid creating a scenario that could cause a defensive rejection. This type of rejection is the result of one party taking a stand (position). Typically, the other party also takes a stand – the opposite one! When two parties take a stand, the result is a standoff. This generates nothing but hot tempers and negative results.

Our prospect responds with just, "no." At this point, most people would begin feeling rejected. They would probably start to develop a negative attitude about their prospect and consequently lose focus on their objective. This could be it for the prospect; but when they say, "no," I suggest you keep going. In many cases the first "no" from a person's mouth is just a reflex. They were only half listening and assumed that your wanting their opinion was the same as asking for a decision. Besides their first objection is often not the real reason behind their saying "no." You need to keep "peeling the onion" to learn their true reason by continuing to ask questions.

To get past this point of the first "no," you need to make a sincere effort to learn more about the person you're talking with. *You need to do your best to understand their position.* Don't proceed without discovering WHY they said, "no." This is a hurdle you need to get over to get to the end gate. If it turns out to be an actual rejection, acknowledge you understand where they're coming from, thank them for their time, and move-on. When you use this method, you'll find an early rejection is less likely to happen.

When In Doubt – Ask A Question

When you're in doubt about what to do next, ask a question. If you would like a detailed response, ask your question in a complimentary fashion. When you say, "I'm sure you have a reason for feeling that way," you need to be careful. You don't want to sound like you're interrogating them. That's why you need to finish your statement with this question – "May I ask what it is?"

The first part, being sure they have a reason, needs to be stated with curiosity and sincerity. You need to genuinely acknowledge they have a reason and you honestly want to know what it is. Be open to the possibility that they may have a different idea. You need to be totally flexible in this regard to present yourself in a friendly way so that they're more likely to share it with you. Then you can offer some reasons why your plan could benefit them more. Regardless of how they're responding, be sure to smile as you're talking to them. Your pleasant attitude will help them relax and be more responsive to you.

Their first "no" may also be a defensive one. They may give you a quick answer that doesn't invite you to pursue the subject, just to put you off. They may not understand exactly what you are proposing, and reject your idea due to their misunderstanding. Yet there is no way at this point for you to determine whether they have presented you with an honest objection or not.

In order to root out real objections from imaginary ones, there is a technique I have used very effectively. Throw their rejection away as nicely as possible. This may mean ignoring it by saying, "We can talk about that later." Or, you can say, "Just suppose, that wasn't the case, then could you see the benefit in my idea (plan, product, service)." If it is real, they will go get it and give it right back to you. They will do this by acknowledging the benefit, but return to their concern or objection. We can always deal with *honest* rejection. Smoke screen rejections do nothing but mislead and get both sides frustrated by the game playing.

How To Nicely Throw Away a Rejection!

Another great way is to start with the word "imagine." When you do, they'll assume you're pretending, and no one ever got hurt while pretending. Then take their rejection and turn it into a positive. If they tell you they don't have enough time say, "Imagine having all the time in the world...." If they complain about not having enough money say, "Imagine if money wasn't an issue...." If they say they don't know anyone they could share the opportunity with say, "Imagine if you had a lot of friends...." Then always finish with the words, "...then could you see the potential?"

If they tell you they don't see the potential of what you've presented, it doesn't matter whether they have enough time or money. If they don't see potential, then there's another reason why they're rejecting what you're offering. You need to ask another question. "I am sure you have another reason. May I ask what it is?" And so on.... As mentioned before, you need to keep "peeling the onion" to get to their true objection.

Zeroing-In On the Real Issue

For now, let's continue as if they say they see the potential but feel time is really an issue. People like to know others understand how they feel. Even though they might not want to admit it, they really enjoy hearing it. So give them what they want and tell them, "I understand." To help them feel even more comfortable with you, say, "I've had others who've also had the same obstacle." You could also use the "feel, felt, found" technique by saying, "I know how you feel. I felt the same way. But here's what I found...." After hearing that, they'll probably want to hear more; so give it to them. If, after your additional explanation, it seems they are ready to reject, ask them another question. "I guess that brings up a question. Is there enough potential in my plan in spite of your concerns about time? Is that the question?"

If they confirm that this truly is the question, you have accomplished two very important things: *First, you have zeroed-in on the real reason for their rejection; it's not just an excuse. This means that you can either deal with it, if possible, or move-on to the next person. The second thing is that you have reduced the rejection to a question. What would you rather do, deal with rejection or answer questions?*

There It Is – Real life

I learned these techniques from some of the top people in this field. And they work. Use them and you are more likely to get the results you want. They will also save you a tremendous amount of time because you will stay on the right path until you get to the bottom of it. You won't be "chasing rainbows" trying to figure out hidden meanings or to see if someone is stalling. This approach also allows the other person to change their mind without losing face. After all, you never really asked them to make a decision one way or the other. You simply asked their opinion on whether or not your plan had potential for them. People can always change their opinion, and given the opportunity, they often do. Give them the chance to turn their "no" into a "yes"!

These techniques will work in any situation; it doesn't have to be business. I've seen it work at home with spouses discussing family issues, neighbors discussing zoning, friends discussing politics, or just about anything that could potentially bring about rejection. Keep in mind, you are there only to present your side of the story.

If you are looking to help someone change their opinion, you need to have them hear the whole story. They need to hear how it'll benefit them to increase the chance they'll join you. If they are rejecting you too soon and the discussion ends before they've been given what they need to make an informed decision, neither one of you will win. In many cases, you just need to keep going. When you use these suggestions, you will generally be able to tell your story. Often, that's the best you can hope for. Even after hearing the whole story, there's no guarantee they'll change their opinion. No matter what though, go for nothing less than doing your best to tell the whole story.

"Anything worth having is worth striving for with all your might."
Orville Redenbacher

"All things are possible to him who believes."
Bible

"The greater the obstacle, the more glory in overcoming it."
Moliere

"God is the silent partner in all great enterprises."
Abraham Lincoln

Part Four

YOUR
UNLIMITED
SKY

Chapter 19

YOU ARE A WONDERFUL
PERSON

The Nineteenth Secret of the NO REJECTION Process

"You need to do your own growing, no matter how tall your grandfather was."
Irish Proverb

Nobody Is Better Than You Are!

One of the reasons many people fear rejection is because, in the past, they have taken it as a personal insult. Rejection is often perceived as devastating to those being rejected. In many cases, they automatically believe the rejection means they are personally deficient in some way. In reality, that's probably not the reason for the rejection at all. The *real fear* of often what is imaginary rejection creates a paralysis against action. It's not really a fear of rejection. It's actually a fear of yourself; fear of failing to do what you said you'd do!

Most people are really *afraid* of what other people think. They're often not consciously aware of this; the fear they feel is so strong it shields their real thoughts. Many people become paralyzed with fear when they *imagine* the reasons they might be rejected. The key word here is *imagine*. Fear of imagined rejection is often so powerful, many people allow it to prevent them from facing their potential rejector. That's sad because that person could have become a great friend, whether they rejected your idea or not. It's your choice. Do you allow fear of yourself, and your ability to handle *imaginary* rejection, prevent you from ever knowing what the outcome would be? As Susan Jeffers says in *Feel the Fear and Do It Anyway,* "Pushing through fear is less frightening than living with the underlying fear that comes from a feeling of helplessness."

Closure – When Do We Need It?

It's the buzzword of the self-help crowd; yet few are using it well. The word is *closure*. It's supposed to mean that you come to a finality in certain situations. For example, suppose you were angry at one of your parents, and they passed away. Attaining closure may require you to write a letter or visit the cemetery to express your true feelings to them. How come you didn't express your anger or love for them while they were alive? It's often the missing piece no one addresses; so the cycle of behavior continues.

People need closure after someone dies because they often had a false fear of rejection while the person was alive. Few people would want to tell a parent they are wrong for fear of losing their love. Yet we are probably able to tell our children or spouse they are way off base in a situation without any such fear. Why? It's often due to a combination of having unintact self-esteem and being intimidated by parental figures. Many of us complain that our parents still treat us like little kids; yet we may still feel the need to have parental approval. It may be something we never totally outgrew. Yet the truth is, wrong is wrong. If someone commits an error, we need to tell them. Whether we do or we don't often depends on our relationship with them.

Be a Good Finder

Sometimes our fear of telling others they may have made an error is based on the *reason* we would tell them, and not the benefit of correcting the error. When we care about someone, we need to point things out to them about their behavior that could help them gain a better understanding and grow as a person. Let's call this "constructive instruction," as criticism only wounds. There's no such thing as constructive criticism! We need to be "good-finders" and compliment them whenever the opportunity presents itself, no matter how small their accomplishment is. Unfortunately, we sometimes make an error known out of anger or in order to turn the focus of attention away from ourselves and our own mistakes.

Why Are Some People So Critical?

Those who are consistently in the habit of pointing out other people's faults, often have a fear of being focused on. They fear the rejection they imagine they would experience if people were to focus on them. Other well-meaning people fear the rejection that, in their minds, is certain to follow any criticism. Yet if you lump all of this together, you are able to focus on and deal with the real fears which have little to do with actual rejection.

All of these people have difficulties because their self-esteem is not intact. They fear rejection and place little value on themselves. They are very self-critical and unhappy with themselves. They are afraid that what they perceive as their true worth is perceived the same way by others. The root of the problem, however, is the lack of respect they *feel* for themselves. They try to view their results and standings in life through an imaginary set of eyes. Instead of looking inside themselves through their own eyes, they take the long way in. They try to look through the eyes of others in an attempt to validate their worth as human beings. This is an unreliable method, to say the least. Like nearsightedness, the more distance you put between your eyes and what you see, the more distorted the picture becomes.

It always seems that these people search for the most critical eyes they can find. They are so convinced they are unworthy that they can't believe it when they see something they accomplish as positive. They keep searching for any flaw they can find. When they succeed at pointing out a weakness, they blow it out of proportion. All of that effort just went to prove to the world how inadequate they believe they really are. They are focusing on their unskillful behavior rather than their skillful behavior. To love the unlovable is the most difficult. But these folks *really* need someone to care about them!

What Other People Think Is *Their* Business

Let go of selfishness and vanity. The people you think are thinking about you, aren't. Most people are too busy thinking about themselves to spend time thinking about you! They don't have time to analyze what you do and why you do it. Just get yourself busy. Get out there and do what you believe needs to be done, and say what needs to be said. Find out who needs help with something – then go help them. Focus on your goals and dreams, while helping others focus on theirs, and you'll get where you're headed.

How do you do that? If you spent your life in fear, how can you overcome it and create a new, positive way of thinking about yourself and your life? Use fear to bring about the changes you want! That's the first step. You need to *really* want to create new results in order to change. Realize that change is not only necessary, but also beneficial and vital to live a happy, healthy, fulfilled life. It took you this long to become who you are and be where you are, and it will also take some time to create a new direction. That's OK. Be patient with the process.

Do the thing you fear, and the fear will disappear! You can do it! You'll then be on your way to a new, more exciting life. As Emerson once said, "Whatever course you decide upon, there is always someone to tell you you're wrong. There are always difficulties arising which tempt you to believe your critics are right. To map out a course of action and follow it to the end requires...courage." Remember, go out on a limb. That's where the fruit is!

How to Use Fear Against Itself

Picture yourself as a mental martial artist. Use the opponent's own weight against them. In this case we'll use fear against itself to help you communicate with someone you care about.

You've held back for years from telling them what you believe they might not want to hear. You're convinced that what you have to say will help them, but you still fear what they will think about you for telling them. You're uneasy about calling attention to this person's behavior for fear they will retaliate by picking apart your shortcomings and rejecting you. You have let your fear of not being able to handle this "carefrontation" stop you from helping this person.

Now for some mental Kung-Fu. What if the information you could share with them during the "carefrontation" would enable them to move-on? What if not telling them, because of your own fear of being rejected, would cause them more pain? How would you feel about yourself if your information would have made a difference in their life, but you refused to share it with them?

To deal with this, you need to be more "afraid" of the results of not telling them, versus telling them. Inaction causes fear to build-up. So take action now! *Tell them what they need to hear, not just what they want to hear.* Congratulations. You have just learned how to use fear against itself, and that's the sign of a leader! Let fear of the results of inaction be greater than the fear of the results of taking action. It works!

Acceptance Brings Responsibility

When I was younger, I was afraid of the responsibility I would have if a girl said, "yes," she would go out on a date with me. I can honestly tell you I never feared being rejected when asking for a date. I never called many girls for a date because I was afraid they'd say "yes"!

My biggest fear was the consequences of acceptance! I was afraid of what I imagined would happen and the increased responsibilities I would have if a girl said, "yes." I was afraid my friends might laugh at me or at the girl I selected. They might make fun of me being more interested in spending time with her, when they wanted me to hang out with them. I might need to make compromises, like going to the dance with her, instead of going to the ballgame with the guys. I could end up part of the "uncool" crowd because she felt sorry for them and wanted us to hang around with them so they would feel better. I'd have no more camping trips. I'd need to get dressed up to eat with her parents when I'd much rather be in comfortable old jeans.

My fear grew so much that I almost started thanking girls if they *wouldn't* go out with me! I'd actually do my best to *invite* rejection! I'd get on the phone and say, "Hi, you wouldn't want to be seen out with me would you?" If one of them said, "yes," I got petrified. Wouldn't you, if you had so many fears?

I wasn't much of an example, was I? *You can have a positive influence on other people as soon as you have one on yourself.* When you focus on the result you want rather than your inner fear, you will enhance your self-esteem and confidence. Just think of all the people you could help by your example. Furthermore, you may also influence some of the bystanders. Some of them would see, by your example, that it's important to focus on your dreams and goals rather than your fears. They'll observe your increased happiness as you help others with your idea, opportunity, product or service. Remember, you can't help someone else without thereby helping yourself! As Ben Sweetland once said, "We cannot hold a torch to light another's path without brightening our own."

The Power of Asking "Why?"

Remember, you are good enough, no matter what anyone tells you or what you tell yourself. However, you do need to believe you are capable of achieving your dreams, coupled with the power of "why?" Kids have this belief early in life and are constantly asking questions. Unfortunately, we may discourage their youthful zeal, confidence, and curiosity. Children often learn more during their first few years than during the rest of their lives! As a young child, do you remember questioning everything? "Why" this and "why" that?

Those of us who are parents may often find ourselves telling our children to stop asking "why?" Unfortunately, after awhile, they may indeed stop. That's why we have a learning curve. During the first few years, the answers to the "whys?" that make some parents "crazy," fill the children with new and exciting knowledge. As some of them are told over and over again to stop asking questions, they sometimes do stop – forever, just to please their parents. They often feel rejected for asking questions and want to avoid future rejection.

Losing the power of "why?" slows the learning process. Once you regain the power of "why?" you can have the learning intensity you once enjoyed as a child. When you begin to ask more questions, you will increase your learning dramatically. You'll also increase your fun! Learning is discovering the newness of things, and that brings excitement. And excited people often live longer and have fuller lives as well. Let rejection trigger the "why?" in you.

Every time you are rejected, ask yourself and the person who rejected you, "why?" The answer could lead to the knowledge that will help you change your approach. Then you'd be able to reduce rejection in the future, or improve your idea or product enough for it to be accepted. This new knowledge can then be expanded by continuing to ask "why?" As we gain more knowledge about ourselves and continue developing our skills, our enthusiasm grows and we want to learn more. To do that, we need to invite the very thing we once feared.

Seek Rejection and You'll Grow

We need to seek rejection in order to grow. Give it your best and expect the best, but don't be attached to the outcome.   If it doesn't turn out the way you want, ask "why?" and say —"Some will, some won't, so what! Who cares?" Fine-tune your skills, shrug off rejection, and keep going. So what if that person said "no." There's a lot more people out there who could say "yes."

We need to return to the time in our youth where the fear of rejection didn't exist and the power of "why?" flourished. Then, and only then, can we begin thoroughly enjoying the excitement of growing again. Only then can we have the most satisfaction in helping others. Our fear has been used against itself and is now under our control.

Fear, like fire, can be used for good when we control it. As Babe Ruth said, "If you want to hit a lot of home runs, you can't worry about striking out." He not only held the home run record for many years; he also struck out more than anyone else in history; a record he still holds!

I believe life *is* a bowl of cherries. Truly successful people get excited about the fruit and use the pits as learning experiences!

> *"I keep six honest serving men*
> *(They taught me all I knew);*
> *Their names are What and Why and When*
> *And How and Where and Who."*
> Rudyard Kipling

> *"Curiosity is one of the permanent and certain*
> *characteristics of a vigorous intellect."*
> Samuel Johnson

Chapter 20

ONLY 15 MINUTES A DAY
The Twentieth Secret of the NO REJECTION Process

"Many times the reading of a book has made the future of a man."

Ralph Waldo Emerson

Reading Can Change Your Life

As mentioned earlier, reading a personal development book for only 15 minutes a day will make a positive difference in your life. It provides insights into how your mind works, and helps you develop discipline and other skills you need to achieve your goals. You'll also read the stories showing you that if the author and others can do it, so can you. Here's a listing of some of the books that are part of my journey, along with some notes explaining how they benefited me and can benefit you too. Reading such books can make a tremendous difference in your life.

The Magic of Thinking Big by David J. Schwartz Ph.D.

Here's some true success secrets.   It taught me the limitless potential of the mind.   I discovered that, with concentrated focus, I can achieve anything I want to.

The 24 Hour Turn-Around by Jim Hartness & Neil Eskelin

Using one hour time periods to read each chapter, I was able to learn that the most difficult step to take when changing is the first one.   Once you take the first step, you gain momentum and anything is possible.   In this book I discovered the power of giving.

Humor is Tremendous, by Charlie "Tremendous" Jones and Bob Phillips

What a bunch of belly laughs! This book is a treasure trove of lighthearted looks at life. Humor is the key to living with a joyful attitude and lifting both your own spirits and the spirits of others. Make people smile and you're sure to be remembered.

Let Go of Whatever Makes You Stop by John L. Mason

Here's 52 little "Nuggets" that will open your eyes to the limits that we all place on ourselves. You will find yourself laughing and using John's one-liners as you go through the book.

Live Your Dreams by Les Brown

I've heard him speak and he writes like he's speaking to you. His heart is in every word. He tells you that if you can dream it then you can be or do it.

Think and Grow Rich by Napoleon Hill

As the title says, think and you can become rich in all areas of your life. I now live with the phrase, "Whatever the mind can conceive, and believe, it can achieve." I read this one at least twice a year!

Personality Plus by Florence Littauer   and *Positive Personality Profiles* by Dr. Robert H. Rohm

In order to develop yourself and effectively communicate with others, you need to understand what type of person you are. To have excellent relationships, you need to understand how to best work with different personalities. Both of these books are owner's manuals for personality understanding and interaction.

How to Win Friends and Influence People by Dale Carnegie

This is the granddaddy of them all! Another must read. It creates a need to understand your affect on other people and tells you what you can do about it.

Chicken Soup for the Soul and A 2nd Helping of Chicken Soup for the Soul by Jack Canfield and Mark Victor Hansen

These inspiring stories will fan that fading spark into a flaming fire of determination to be a full-time human being, who makes a difference every day.

Storms of Perfection by Andy Andrews

The letters in this book from well-known people taught me that if these people can survive and prosper through oftentimes devastating rejection, so can all of us. What we see when we observe these people who rose to the top, is often just the signs of their success. Their letters show the rejection they dealt with along the way.

No Excuse! — A New Philosophy for Overcoming Obstacles & Achieving Excellence by Jay Rifenbary

No whining, blaming, or complaining! Get on with it. This principled centered, action oriented, fascinating book will captivate and educate you, while lifting your spirits. It taught me my power to succeed comes directly from taking personal responsibility for everything in my life. It made me realize that I am the master of my own destiny and taught me how to make it happen.   Living by the No Excuse! Philosophy has made a difference in my life.

Brighten Your Day With Self-Esteem by William J. McGrane

Self-Esteem is the respect you feel for yourself, and it determines the quality of your life. Do you feel enough respect for yourself to do whatever it takes to give yourself and your family the life you want?   I learned that by increasing my self-esteem my confidence went up and my fear of rejection went down. Self-esteem is vital to your success. Incorporate these principles into your life and as Bill says, "Watch what happens."

These are just a few of the many titles out there to help you on your journey of success. If you find one book that seems to make more of a difference in you than others, I recommend you make it a point to re-read it as often as you can. Each time you do, you'll benefit more because you'll have a new level of understanding. As bestselling author and speaker, Charlie "Tremendous" Jones says, "The greatest difference in your life over the next five years will be in the books you read and the people you meet." Read any good books lately? Met any great people?

"Books have meant to my life what the sun has meant to planet earth."
Earl Nightingale

"There is more treasure in books than in all the pirates' loot on Treasure Island...and best of all, you can enjoy these riches every day of your life."
Walt Disney

"Setting aside just 15 minutes a day will enable you to read up to two dozen books a year. Keep it up and you will have read 1,000 books in your lifetime. That's the equivalent of going to college five times."
G. Gordan

U

Chapter 21

UNDYING GRATITUDE & HOPE
The Twenty-first Secret of the NO REJECTION Process

"The only place success comes before work is in the dictionary."
Vidal Sassoon

An Attitude of Gratitude

I hope your reading this book has helped you understand you are not alone – that everyone gets rejected along the road of success. It's important to be grateful for all the lessons we've learned along the line. Some have come disguised as rejection and may have been painful. Yet, when we allow ourselves to have an attitude of gratitude, we can acknowledge that the most difficult rejections we received resulted in our greatest growth. We decided to be better rather than bitter.

Has this information been helpful to you? Are your dreams growing stronger? Did you know your dreams bring out your greatness? If I have helped you, even in some small way, that's reward enough for me.

If you feared the unknown before you read this book, and now you approach each new day with appreciation as a path to discovery, that's terrific. I applaud you for being committed to your personal development and for the contributions you'll continue to make to the world.

Thank you for allowing me to spend what precious little time we have together, sharing an idea or two. It's much easier working toward a goal together rather than alone. The *Bible* says that as one we can do 1,000 but as two we can do 10,000. There's incredible strength in numbers. If you have increased your numbers, that's wonderful.

As long as ideas get shared with other people, they stay alive and thrive. If you got and applied just one idea from this book, share it with someone else so they can grow too. You'll feel good about it, and they may even thank you for it!

My goal with this book is to help others with the knowledge and experience I've gained over the years. I believe I can do this best by writing about real life and helping people achieve their birthright; their true greatness. To think I could accomplish this alone would be far from the truth. We all need to work together to support each other. As Robert H. Schuller says, "I can tell you how to succeed, but I can't tell you how to succeed alone."

To become teachers of greatness we all need a mentor to teach us how to bring out the greatness we were born with. Then we need to pass it on, teaching others to do the same.

Together we can accomplish whatever we set our minds to. We can all make a difference, large or small, in the world.

Turning Rejection Into Direction

Successful people have generally been rejected many times on their journey of success. This letter from Andy Andrews' book *Storms of Perfection* is a case in point. It shows what results can come from dealing with rejection.

Dear Andy,

When I graduated from Columbia University, the Dean of Announcers for NBC Radio, Pat Kelly, told me that even though I had the best well-modulated voice for broadcasting, I should go out and get a job as a secretary or a receptionist – they weren't using women. That's when I first became acquainted with the "R" word – "Rejection."

I look back on that time and I have to laugh. It made me more determined than ever to accomplish in my chosen field.

Eighteen firings later somehow, like the Peter Principle, I always got fired "up" — and was more determined than ever to be successful. When I came up through the ranks, I came up when women were not on the air and still did not have a presence on radio or television. So I was facing even greater competition – men! Through all of these firings, I always felt that I was right – and they (the bosses) were wrong. I had to – in order to be successful; I took that rejection and turned it into direction. By the way, some of these were justified.

After spending a lifetime of talking from every perspective, I've recognized a number of patterns emerging. The more people I come in contact with, the more information I have on living my life – and, the more information I have to turn around and share with others.

Have I gotten used to rejection? Absolutely not. It's taken me a long time to learn how to handle the rejection of my firings – to balance – to know that it was all right to be in the top 10% – to forgive myself for not being number one, and to <u>endure</u>. Have I used it to become an accomplished broadcaster and television talk show host? Yes! Would I do it again, the same way? You're damn right! That's how I got where I am today.

Sincerely,
Sally Jessy Raphael

Hope Can Lead to Miracles

As I finish this book, I am thinking of a story that was just on the news. A police officer was in a coma for seven years. By some miracle, he woke up. It was all over the TV networks. In the morning, one show had a doctor on as a guest. He was an expert on comas. The doctor wanted to make it very clear that the true fact was, this man probably wasn't in a coma. He felt this information would keep families of other coma patients from getting their hopes up!

He wanted to keep people from getting their hopes up? My dear doctor, hope is what keeps us going. As Robert H. Schuller says, "There is no false hope." Hope is hope! The medical field often tries to downplay the miracle angle. But, isn't it a miracle that families have enough hope to come together and pray for the recovery of loved ones who seem forever lost in a coma? When someone recovers from a dangerous illness and looks at the rest of their lives as a second chance, I call that a miracle. When a baby is born with physical or mental challenges and the parents find a love inside themselves they never experienced before, I doubt science can explain that as anything less than a miracle.

Miracles happen every day; expect them to happen to you, and show gratitude when they come. *Turn rejection into direction, and you'll gain the advantage that leads to ultimate acceptance.* Go forward in faith, face your fears of rejection, deal with them, and move-on. Do this and you can make your dreams come true.

About the Author

John Fuhrman is first and foremost a husband and father. He is also a speaker, peak performance trainer, and consultant. He is founder and president of *Frame of Mind*, an organization dedicated to the motivation and performance enhancement of all clients. He has been an award winning sales producer and manager and entrepreneur. He is a current member of the National Speakers Association, and has been featured in *Selling Magazine* as an authority on rejection.

Through large doses of personal experience, coupled with humor, John has enhanced the performance of hundreds of sales and business professionals. He is a sought after speaker and author on success, motivation, management and team building, as well as leadership and networking. He lives with his wife, Helen, and their two children, John and Katie.

RULES OF REJECTION

REACH FOR HIGHER GROUND AND THEY SLAP YOUR HANDS... KEEP REACHING.

EXPECT TO BE SUCCESSFUL AND THEY CALL YOU A DREAMER... DREAM ON.

JUMP AT A GOOD OPPORTUNITY AND BE LABELED UNSTABLE... JUMP HIGHER.

EVERYTHING HAPPENS FOR A REASON ...YOU BE THE REASON.

CHALLENGE THE NORM AND BE LABELED A REBEL...LEAD A REBELLION.

TOLERANCE IS OFTEN MISTAKEN FOR WEAKNESS...BE TOLERANT ANYWAY.

IDEAS SPROUT FROM THE SEEDS OF REJECTION...GO GET REJECTED.

OPEN YOUR HEART TO MINDS THAT HAVE CLOSED...TAKE JOY IN THEIR OPENING.

NOTICE A STRENGTH IN EVERYONE YOU MEET...YOU WILL BECOME STRONGER.

Before starting your day, visualize yourself "as if" you had already followed the "RULES." What type of person do you become? Do you like how it feels? What if everyone felt this way? Like the game of life, the true enjoyment comes from following the rules regardless of what the other players do.

The best way to learn is to teach. When you spend your days living and teaching these rules, your world will be a better place. Do it with intensity for thirty days and you will see successes you've never imagined. Always remember, you can't help another without thereby helping yourself.

NOTES

NOTES

NOTES

NOTES